Choose
to
Learn

Teaching for
SUCCESS
Every Day

Russell T. Osguthorpe • Lolly S. Osguthorpe

Skyhorse Publishing

Skyhorse Publishing books may be purchased in bulk at special discounts for sales promotion, corporate gifts, fund-raising, or educational purposes. Special editions can also be created to specifications. For details, contact the Special Sales Department, Skyhorse Publishing, 307 West 36th Street, 11th Floor, New York, NY 10018 or info@skyhorsepublishing.com.

Skyhorse® and Skyhorse Publishing® are registered trademarks of Skyhorse Publishing, Inc.®, a Delaware corporation.

Visit our website at www.skyhorsepublishing.com.

10 9 8 7 6 5 4 3 2 1

Library of Congress Cataloging-in-Publication Data is available on file.

Cover design by Monique Hahn

Print ISBN: 978-1-63450-316-7
Ebook ISBN: 978-1-5107-0088-8

Printed in China

Choose to Learn

*To our children, who continue to teach us
that we can always choose to learn.*

Contents

Preface

In a way we have been writing this book our whole lives. Lolly is a sixth-grade teacher. Russ is a university professor. We are parents of five children and grandparents of sixteen grandchildren. It is in living these roles that the principles in this book have emerged. Some would say that we have been "researching our own lived experience," a method of making meaning by reflecting on one's life (e.g., Van Manen, 1990). Others might say that we have been conducting studies in "appreciative inquiry," an approach that helps improve whole organizations by focusing on their core strengths (Cooperrider & Whitney, 2005). Still others might conclude that we have drawn from accepted theories in psychology or sociology such as self-efficacy theory (Bandura, 1997).

This volume might be viewed as a book to improve teaching and learning, a self-help book, or a guide to improve the performance of an entire school. We are not concerned about which view readers take; we simply want to achieve one central purpose: helping readers go beyond where they have gone before—doing better than they thought they could do—and in the process, helping others do the same. This is the central message of this book, and it applies to educators and those they educate—such as teachers, principals, and students—but it also applies to parents and families. We believe that this broad application is possible because the principles we describe in this book are fundamental to human improvement.

THE MODEL

This book is organized around a model that we call Choose to Learn. This model consists of eight principles that lead to *success* (the first principle). The remaining principles are *urgency, risk, passion, help, motives, faith,* and *leadership.* By the time you finish the book, these one-word descriptors will help you remember each of the principles we include in the book and will serve as reminders of how you can use these principles to help students and other teachers.

Everything in the model is based on an individual's power to make personal choices—decisions that lead one closer to or further away from learning. That is why the illustration of the model at the beginning of each chapter is surrounded by the words "The Power of Personal Agency." If someone were to ask us about the theoretical premise of the book, we would explain that every diagram, every table, every illustration rests on that one premise: the power of personal agency. Our purpose is to help every reader magnify that power and use it to benefit others.

APPLYING THE MODEL

A model or an idea is valuable only to the degree that it is practiced. So many potential advances in education are ineffective not because the ideas are useless but because the ideas are not used. To help readers use the ideas in this book, we have included at the end of each chapter a section titled "Making It Happen." This section contains suggestions for teachers to use the principles in each chapter to help students become more successful in their learning. Each suggestion is based on real experience with real students in real classrooms. Because we have used these suggestions in our own teaching, we are confident that when you use them, you will see marked improvement in student learning.

We do not see the lists of ideas in the Making It Happen sections as exhaustive. Instead, they are a way for teachers to begin experimenting with the principles that flow out of each part of the model.

Author Web Site

We invite all readers to share with us your ideas for implementing the model. Some of these ideas will focus on how you used the model in the classroom. Others will emphasize personal applications of the model in your own life. To share an idea or learn about others' ideas, simply go to the following Web site: http://choosetolearn.net/. In addition to a readers' forum, the site will contain podcasts of the authors describing how to use the principles in the book to help students and others choose to learn.

Helping Everyone Become a Learner

There are few things in life more exciting than doing better than we've done before. Life, in one sense, is a series of learning experiences. The more we learn about ourselves and about the world around us, the better our life becomes—but only if we *succeed* in these learning experiences. If the challenges we face in the classroom or in the home or in our private space overwhelm us, we learn about defeat and may in the process become addicted to it. Then we become less able to face the next difficulty that comes. However, if we overcome the challenges, we learn about victory and become stronger and more certain that we can accomplish whatever goal we may set.

We agree with Benjamin Barber, a renowned sociologist, who said, "I don't divide the world into the weak and the strong, or the successes and the failures. . . . I divide the world into the *learners and nonlearners*" (see Dweck, 2006, p. 16; emphasis added). The person who chooses not to learn—and to avoid a task because it is too daunting—chooses not to live life to its fullest. The one who says, "This is good enough, I don't need to do any better," never feels the sensation of overcoming the seemingly impossible. This book is about helping oneself and others become learners by feeling those sensations every day.

Note: When we share stories from our own experience, we will use first person. Accounts of younger learners are usually Lolly's, while those of adult students are Russ's.

Acknowledgments

Most who have contributed to this book have done so indirectly, not knowing that they were the ones who "lit our fire." Our children taught us and continue to teach us that the power to choose is in each one of us. Our missionaries taught us that everyone can succeed and that faith works. Our students teach us daily that we can all do better than we think we can do. And our parents taught us never to give up. To all of these we owe a debt that we can never completely repay. And to those who have helped us directly, we also give thanks: Mary May Osguthorpe, for her talents in graphic artwork and her eagerness to offer those talents; Debbie Stollenwerk and Allison Scott for their enthusiasm, encouragement, and thoughtful suggestions; Mary Tederstrom and Libby Larson for their careful editing of the final manuscript; as well as all of the reviewers who gave helpful suggestions on early drafts of the book:

Michael J. Butts
High School Principal
Watertown School District 200 Ninth St NE
Watertown, South Dakota

Lori L. Grossman
Instructional Coordinator, New Teacher Induction and
    Mentoring, Professional Development Services
Houston Independent School District
Houston, Texas

Barbara Hayhurst
Special Education Teacher
Vallivue School District
Caldwell, Idaho

Pauline H. Jacroux
Retired First Grade Teacher
Kailua, Hawai'i

Susan Kessler, EdD
Assistant Principal
Hillsboro High School
Nashville, Tennessee

Renee Peoples, NBCT
Fourth Grade Teacher/Math Coach
West Elementary/Swain County
Bryson City, North Carolina

Steve Reifman
Elementary School Teacher
Roosevelt School, Santa Monica
Santa Monica, California

Marilyn Steneken
Middle School Teacher
Sparta, New Jersey

Charre Todd
District Science Coach
Crossett Public Schools
Crossett, Arkansas

Stephen Valentine
English Department Chair
Montclair Kimberley Academy
Montclair, New Jersey

About the Authors

Russell T. Osguthorpe, professor of instructional psychology and technology, currently serves as director of the Center for Teaching and Learning at Brigham Young University. He has also served as chair of his department and associate dean of the David O. McKay School of Education. In 1998 he was awarded the Martha Jane Knowlton Corey University Professorship. Prior to joining Brigham Young University, he served on the faculty of the National Technical Institute for the Deaf in Rochester, New York. He speaks several languages; has collaborated on educational projects in China, Europe, and Polynesia; and has been a visiting scholar at the University of Toronto and the University of Paris. He has authored five books and more than fifty journal articles on instructional design, teacher education, and special education.

Lolly S. Osguthorpe currently teaches sixth grade at Rock Canyon Elementary School in Provo, Utah. With a background in early childhood education and elementary education, including a minor in music, she taught preschool, tutored young reading and math students, and coached voice and piano students of all ages. In the past she served as president of the PTA and on school and community councils. She has held numerous teaching and leadership positions in children's, youth, and women's organizations.

The Osguthorpes are the parents of five children and the grandparents of sixteen grandchildren. They are both former members of the Mormon Tabernacle Choir and other community chorals. They reside in Provo, Utah.

Introduction

Education does not become exciting until both learners and teachers accomplish what they previously thought was impossible. I once taught voice lessons to a teenage boy, Jason, who came to me with no musical gifts. When he began his lessons, he could not match pitch and could not produce a pleasing vocal tone, but he wanted to learn how to sing. In addition to the difficulties he had with singing, he also had a severe reading disability. At first I wondered if Jason would succeed. Listening to him was so painful (a little like chalk squeaking on a blackboard) that our children usually left the house during his lessons.

But patiently I worked with him until he gained the ability to sing the notes I played on the piano. Finally, after months of practice, he performed a memorized medley of songs before an audience of some four hundred people. Together Jason and I accomplished what both had previously thought was impossible. Gradually our expectations for ourselves and for each other changed, and the success we sought finally arrived.

This is a book about teaching for success every day. It is not about helping students or teachers become satisfied by meeting minimum requirements from the district or state. Rather, it is a book about how to go beyond these merely acceptable levels of learning. It is about helping teachers and learners alike rise together, reaching heights that they may never have reached before.

The principles we offer in this book have been proven in practice with young learners as well as with adult learners. The principles work with all age groups because they are fundamental to all successful human endeavors. Identify a school, a class, or an individual that has significantly exceeded minimum acceptable standards of performance, and you will see the principles in this book in action. Perhaps those experiencing the success did not name the principles the way we will name them, but the principles are at the heart of the successful venture nonetheless. By naming them and showing how they affect both teaching and learning, we hope to make them more accessible and easier to use by anyone who reads this book.

My voice student, Jason, not only accomplished his original goal of learning how to sing but also improved his reading skills, his social skills, and his ability to attack new learning challenges. He gained the courage to sing in front of a large audience without the sound of fear in his voice. He achieved all of this by constantly trying to do his best. And the more he did his best, the better his best became. Likewise, as I kept searching for new approaches to help him, my best also improved. The process relied most importantly on changing the expectations of both learner and teacher. Both Jason and I began to expect success, and success came. This book is about how to help that kind of learning and teaching happen more often.

What Is Success?

We asked a group of teachers recently to define success from a student's point of view: "How do students know when they've succeeded?" Their responses were revealing. One said, "Getting an A." Another: "Learning everything the teacher taught." All of the responses were ultimately limiting. None was inspiring. How lofty a goal is it, after all, to get a good grade? What does that grade really mean? Is it possible to get an A and not learn very much? Of course it is. Is it possible to "learn everything the teacher taught" and still not learn a lot? Yes, especially when the teacher doesn't teach very much. Success for a public school administrator might be for students to score at grade level on the state core tests, but this definition is not very uplifting and would not infuse a student or a teacher with new energy, more motivation, or increased confidence.

Our definition of success does not focus on meeting minimum standards, whether those standards be grades, test scores, or state mandates. Rather, our definition rests on changes that occur inside the learner and teacher, changes that lead to higher levels of performance than either one of them has previously imagined. Success is being empowered to do what one previously thought was impossible, and then to keep on progressing far beyond anything previously attained. In the field of organizational studies, one of the most well-documented theories shows that as personal expectations increase, human performance rises at a predictable rate (David Whetten, personal communication, August 13, 2007). Expectations affect performance in a positive and predictable way, and then performance reciprocates to positively affect expectations. The two keep pushing each other up. Success, then, is when these two forces keep working on each other, and the learner or teacher continues to rise beyond previous levels of performance.

With our definition, success is not a static goal to be reached. It is dynamic and ever changing. Imagine the pole vaulter jumping over the bar. Success is not clearing the bar and then congratulating oneself. The bar actually keeps rising, and the athlete keeps expecting to clear it. Now, one might say that in this example there is a clear limit. A person can jump only so high, but if one examines pole vault records historically, it becomes clear that the bar has kept rising. For example, in 1912, the world record pole vault height was 4.02 meters. In 1963 the record was 5.00 meters. In 2006, 6.00 meters, and it continues to rise. What was once seen as completely impossible becomes the norm. The records are broken over and over again. Of course, the sport changes, the equipment changes, the athletes become more skilled. The point is that reaching minimum levels is not the definition of success in this sport or any other. It's going beyond where one has gone before.

WHAT IS FAILURE?

If success is going beyond the norm—exceeding one's personal best—what is failure? It is being satisfied with the present, just the way it is, with no improvement at all. Our definition of failure does not infer that one must regress. Rather, one must simply refuse to get better. It is not only falling short of the mark; it is refusing even to try to reach the mark. But what is the mark? Who sets it? In this book the mark is based on expectations. Failure cannot occur in the absence of expectations, but whose expectations? The teacher's? The parent's? The district's? The state's?

When a student develops a pattern of failure, it doesn't matter who is setting the expectations. A student who is addicted to failure falls short of everyone's mark because the student has developed a deep-seated belief that success is impossible. This belief—the student's own expectations—is the most important determinant of all. A student who becomes entrapped in such an addiction—the addiction to unbelief or low expectations—continues to perform poorly year after year and never discovers how good success can taste. Our purpose in this book is to propose realistic ways for educators to help others overcome these addictions to failure by choosing to learn.

Anytime one learns, one succeeds. Anytime one refuses to learn, one fails. Learning and success are inseparable. To learn does not mean to claw one's way up to the edge of the cliff and hang on for dear life. It means to get on top of the mountain, stand there, and look around at all that now awaits. Learning is an invitation to the next peak. Failure is saying, "I don't want to climb that mountain. I'm not a good climber. I will probably fall. I'll just stay down here at the bottom and wait for you." The person is choosing—choosing to fail. We are making a case in this book for helping students, teachers—generally everyone—choose success by choosing to learn.

1

The Three D's of Success

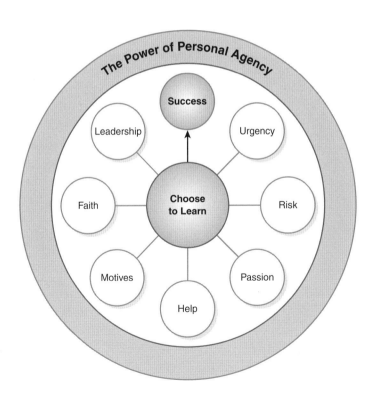

Slightly overweight and somewhat awkward, Shawn liked video games more than real games, even though he wasn't very good at either. After school he went downstairs, closed his bedroom door, chose a game on his computer, and tried to make it to the next level. He didn't feel comfortable with most people, especially adults. He hated his fourth-grade teacher. She just asked him to do things he didn't want to do. Like reading. Computer images he could handle, but words were not his thing. Still reading on the first-grade level, books were intimidating, and his life didn't get much better as he went from elementary to secondary school. We actually met him when he was nineteen. We asked him one day if he had ever succeeded at anything—"skateboarding, skiing, anything?" Afraid to look us in the eye, he mumbled, "No." We then told him that his days of constant failure were over: "You're going to see what it feels like to succeed."

Shawn is like so many of our young people. Each year the Commissioner for the National Center for Educational Statistics produces a report about the state of education in the United States. In the spring of 2007 his report showed that fourth and eighth graders' reading ability has varied little during the past fifteen years. Fewer than one-third of the students performed at the proficient level, and twelfth graders' reading performance has decreased significantly, from 40 percent to 35 percent at the proficient level.

Likewise, fully 39 percent of these twelfth graders in 2005 performed below the "basic" level in mathematics. This means that at the end of their high school education these students did not even possess "partial mastery of fundamental skills."

How did students do in science? Quite similarly. The fourth graders showed some improvement during the past ten years, the eighth graders stayed the same, and the twelfth graders did worse. So it appears that even when students show slight gains in the early grades in reading, math, or science, those gains eventually lead to deficits by the time the students graduate from high school (see Schneider, 2007).

What happens to students as they complete a college education? Again, the data are deeply disappointing. Romano (2005) laments that only 31 percent of college graduates in 2003 read at the proficient level, significantly down from 40 percent ten years earlier. The one clear conclusion from all the data on education, the No Child Left Behind Act, and undergraduate education in the United States is that we are not improving. Policies and programs the nation has implemented to raise literacy rates in reading, math, or science are not working. In short, most students are not succeeding. Many are graduating and getting degrees, but they are not succeeding, because their desire to learn has weakened and diminished rather than grown stronger and brighter.

We argue that addiction to failure is one of the primary causes of such disappointing results from our system of education. Shawn was obviously addicted to failure. He did not expect to succeed at anything he tried. There may have been some teachers in his life who were also addicted to failure— teachers who did not expect to succeed with Shawn when he was in their class. There might also have been parents, administrators, and policymakers with similar addictions. Why? Because they were not experiencing success in their role— whatever that role was. Those in leadership positions who develop addictions to failure express their frustration in cynical remarks.

A Chinese student once asked me to define the word *cynic*. I read her the dictionary definition: "one who believes that human conduct is motivated wholly by self-interest" (*Merriam Webster's Collegiate Dictionary, Tenth Edition*). A cynic is someone who always focuses on the negative. Cynics, in fact, are *addicted* to the negative. One of our favorite remarks about cynicism follows: "When I was a young man and was prone to speak critically, my father would say: 'Cynics do not contribute, skeptics do not create, doubters do not achieve'" (Hinckley, 1986, p. 2).

Students can fall prey to cynicism but so can teachers and educational leaders. Just listen sometime to educators talk about the policies that govern their practice. The policies might be at the school, district, state, or national level, but rather than focusing on legitimate flaws in a policy and suggesting strategies to improve it, the conversation often turns toward hopelessness and pessimism.

What we offer in this chapter is an alternative to cynicism, a way out of negativism, an antidote for failure: we call it the Three D's of Success—*desire, decision,* and *determination.* We are convinced that when teachers, students, and leaders practice the Three D's, addictions to failure and negativism gradually disappear, and learning for everyone—both students and teachers—increases.

DESIRE

The first "D" in the success equation is *desire.* As Mager and Pipe (1997) put it, "you really oughta wanna." If students don't want to learn, they won't learn. If teachers don't want to improve, they won't improve. If leaders don't have the will to change and help others change, everything will remain the same or worsen. Desire must be present. The word *desire,* however, can be viewed in several ways. Many focus on its emotional meaning—a longing, a yearning, an attraction. We define *desire* quite differently.

When we speak of desire in this book, we are emphasizing the end result of the word. For us the most apt synonym for desire is the word *goal.* The person wants to *do* something or *be* something. A student might want to learn how to read well enough to read the Harry Potter books. This is a definitive goal, and the goal itself is the best expression of the student's desire. Using this definition, the word *desire* is no longer simply an emotion that we cannot get our arms around. It's a thought, an aim, a determiner of personal conduct. Figure 1.1 shows that desire is the beginning of success.

Notice that below the word *desire* is the phrase *Think about it.* Whatever a student or teacher is thinking about is the most powerful determinant of what that student or teacher will do.

Figure 1.1   Desire

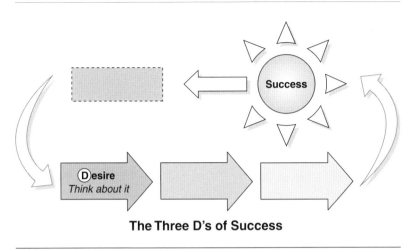

The Three D's of Success

"We are always moving in the direction of our most dominant thought" (Waitley, 1985, p. 126). Another way of saying that is: "Our thinking determines our behavior." The thing we *desire* most or *think about* most—our *goal*—will always drive our actions. So when a student laments, "I really don't have any desire. I don't want to do anything right now," as educators we should not believe the student. It's actually not true. The student wants to do *something*. We just don't know what that something is, and the student might not know either. The only way to proceed is to go to the next step in the three D's—to help the student *decide* to do something.

DECISION

A teacher typically reacts to a student who is lethargic by trying to identify the underlying cause of the malaise—then, supposedly, desire will increase and the student will be reenergized. We assert that there is a more effective way of motivating seemingly impossible to motivate students: helping them do the task at hand, helping them decide to perform— even if they don't feel any desire at the moment. The principle upon which the Three D's is built is that desire will increase following success. The idea is akin to what Albert Bandura calls "the empowerment model" (Evans, 1989, p. 16). So as educators we don't need to waste time trying to pump up students' desire while waiting for them to become engaged in the learning task. The learning task itself—if it is designed effectively—will do the pumping up automatically. Helping students set goals that they want to achieve is much easier than psychoanalyzing each student's lack of desire.

So once students have defined the goals they want to achieve, they then must *decide* to achieve them. The student who wanted to improve his reading ability so he could read a Harry Potter book must now decide to *do* things that will lead to the achievement of that goal. This is where the educator has the most power to influence learning: helping the student set realistic, appropriate learning goals that will lead to the accomplishment of the student's desired outcome. Bandura (1994) calls this type of instruction "guided mastery."

Students who are addicted to failure never really decide to do anything. They sit and wait for the teacher to direct them. Teachers or educational leaders who are addicted to failure likewise avoid making the decisions they need to make (decisions that involve risk) because they are afraid of failure. For example, they implement district or state mandates without deciding how those mandates can actually benefit specific students in their classroom or school. Figure 1.2 shows that *decision* is the second step toward success.

A noneducation example helps illustrate our point. The American Heart Association (2007) reports that more than four out of five smokers wish they could quit. So when they say, "I'm addicted," a friend might ask: "Do you really want to stop?" "Oh yes, but I've tried, and I can't." The next question the friend could pose is: "Have you ever actually *decided* to stop?" Most smokers will admit that they can't bring themselves to make the decision. One smoker described it to us this way, "There's still something inside me that wants to keep smoking." In other words, "I can't go against my own desire, so I just won't make the decision to stop, because there's

Figure 1.2   Decision

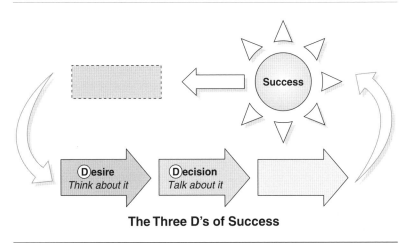

The Three D's of Success

always the chance that my inner desire might take over again and cause me to smoke." As Schaler (2000) asserts in his book by the same title, "Addiction is a choice." We recognize that genetic tendencies can predispose people to certain types of addictions, but we assert that people still have power over their own conduct. They can choose to overcome an addiction to failure. They can choose to succeed.

Students and teachers are not very different from the smoker who avoids making a decision to quit. Every human being is born with a powerful inner strength: the power to choose, or the power of personal agency. It is the most important attribute anyone possesses. A student can choose to focus her attention on the teacher or on a book or on a text message that just arrived. A teacher can choose to focus his attention on helping a student overcome a hurdle or on how to avoid the next inservice meeting. The power of choice is always with us, and that power is far greater than most realize. When one exercises this inner power, one begins *talking about it,* as shown in Figure 1.2. Decision making is more than the thought process identified in the *desire* stage of the Three D's. When we make a decision, we eventually share it with someone else.

The example of Shawn, the young adult with a reading disability, points to the power of talking about one's decision. He had to decide to change. He had to decide to submit himself to a peer tutor who wanted to help him. He had to decide to try, and not until he made those decisions public (to "talk about it" with his tutor and others), did he see any success. Deciding can be a scary thing. When anyone decides on a new course of action, an old way of being must be left behind. After becoming more proficient in reading, Shawn could no longer describe himself as "disabled." He might still have felt the effects of learning problems he had suffered in the past, but he could no longer accept sympathy from others because of his difficulty with reading. Why? Because he became more proficient at the task. He *decided* to change. He exercised his personal power of agency to *do* something different and to *be* someone different. As he made these decisions, he began talking to others about them.

In this book, when we discuss personal agency or the power to choose, we are talking about a particular kind of choice making. *Educare,* the Latin root of the word *education,* means to "draw out." The process of education, then, is to draw out the good that is already inside students—to amplify the positive characteristics, talents, and abilities that define them. So as educators help students make a decision, the quality of the decision matters. It is not just a process of helping students make *any* decision, good or bad. It is trying to draw out the good (see Hansen, 2001). It is helping students learn how to make decisions that empower them to be more effective contributors to society. The addict makes decisions every day to remain addicted. An effective teacher is one who helps others make decisions that lead them away from harmful addictions, particularly the addiction to failure.

DETERMINATION

The process of leading others away from harmful behavior and toward a worthy goal demands determination. This is the third of the Three D's. This is the hard work part of success.

This occurs when a student cannot resist the pull to move toward that good goal. The student or teacher has progressed beyond "thinking about it" and "talking about it." Now it's time to *do* it, as shown in Figure 1.3.

Figure 1.3   Determination

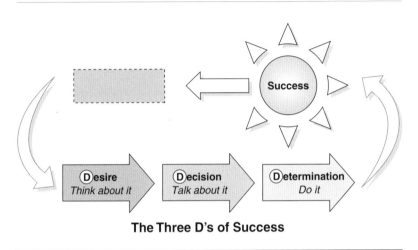

The Three D's of Success

The story of Coach Jim Ellis's swim team in inner city Philadelphia shows the effects of determination, as depicted in the movie *Pride* (see Rainer, 2007). With their recreation center about to be shut down, Coach Ellis invited a group of young people who lacked direction in their lives to become swimmers. During their first swim meet they lost every race to the opposing team. Then on the way back home, they joked about their opponents and made light of their own failure.

Coach Ellis then gave them a stern lecture and asked if they wanted to change or if they wanted to continue to experience failure as they always had. He chastised them for making light of their own poor performance and helped them face reality. The next day they all came to the pool ready to work, ready to *do it*. They became *determined* not only as swimmers but as students. With Ellis as their guide, their determination paid off. Their skills developed. Their confidence increased, and their ability to win meets changed dramatically. They eventually placed first in a national swim meet, and some of the team members went on to enter the Olympic trials.

This coach and his swimmers developed an understanding of the Three D's of Success. They had a *desire,* expressed as a goal: to win meets. They exercised their personal agency by *deciding* to give up unproductive ways of behaving and trade them in for more effective ways. They then became relentlessly *determined* to succeed, and every time they succeeded, their expectations rose. As their expectations rose, their desire to achieve more also increased. Coach Ellis did not need to infuse them with new desire. The desire came naturally as their expectations expanded. They knew they could achieve what they had achieved at the previous meet, and so they then wanted or *desired* to achieve more so they could advance to the next level.

EXPECTATIONS

The *Expectations* box in Figure 1.4 is perhaps the most critical part of the Three D's model. This model focuses primarily on the expectations of the learner. Until students' expectations of themselves increase, their performance will remain the same. We are not referring to a mercurial type of hope that comes and goes. When we say *expectation,* we mean a firm belief that the goal will be achieved (see Bandura, 1994). Given that the goal is something that the student has never achieved before, such expectations can be daunting. Because the former goal has already been achieved—however small that goal was—the new goal is clearly attainable. We talk more in later chapters about how the teacher's expectations also rise as a result of students' expectations rising.

If you begin examining your own conduct as an educator, you will see how apparent each of the Three D's is in your own life, as well as in the lives of your students—simple yet powerful. When a student is failing, that student is lacking in one or more of the Three D's. When students are succeeding, they are following the complete path outlined in Figure 1.4.

Figure 1.4   Expectations

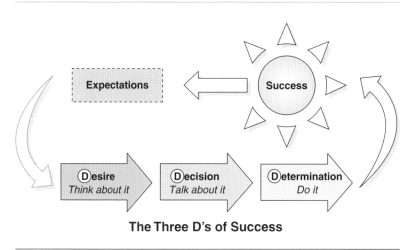

The Three D's of Success

Each student experiences the Three D's differently. One student may have the most difficulty with the decision phase, while another may struggle most with determination. Each may need a different type of help while moving through the Three D's, but each of the D's is present when someone is continuing to improve. The model constitutes a tool that teachers can use every day in their practice. Whether the student is a young child, an adolescent, or an adult, the Three D's apply equally to all.

The power of the model is that it proposes a way to lift the unmotivated student. Rather than searching for reasons for a student's poor performance, the teacher helps the student set achievable goals, make decisions to go after those goals, become determined to achieve the goals, and finally attain success. By focusing on a student's self-generated success, expectations increase, desire grows, personal agency expands, and determination strengthens. It is a cyclical process, as Figure 1.4 illustrates. The student who succeeds once wants to succeed again and again.

When a student is not progressing through the cycle of the Three D's, the student becomes susceptible to an addiction to failure. How can a teacher recognize such a tendency? Simply think of the Three D's cycle in reverse. When a student lacks desire, has trouble making a decision to accomplish a task, and gives up easily, the student's expectations decrease, desire suffers, decisions become even more difficult, and determination evaporates. When these symptoms become apparent, the student is at risk for developing an addiction to failure.

APPLYING THE THREE D'S OF SUCCESS

At the beginning of the school year, Samantha, a sixth-grade student, scored in the fourth percentile on a national comprehension exam. The results of the criterion-referenced test also showed serious deficiencies in reading, language, and comprehension. She appeared to have attention deficit disorder (ADD) but was always well-behaved and often tried very hard to stay on task even though it was difficult for her.

When I presented her parents with the facts, they agreed to have her tested but were reluctant to consider medication for ADD. Even though her test scores were low, the results of the entire battery of assessments showed that she did not qualify for special education services. Her parents had a deep desire to help her improve but did not know exactly how to proceed. I trained the parents to tutor Samantha every day for one hour. The training focused on comprehension strategies taught in school. I also administered extra comprehension quizzes to Samantha at school and helped her select books that were below sixth-grade level—books that would ensure incremental success. I also worked with her for a few minutes each day on vocabulary and comprehension skills in addition to regular classroom instruction on reading. Each time Samantha experienced success—which was often—her desire to try harder increased and she became more determined.

The family carried out its commitment, and every week Samantha took a comprehension test on each book she read. Success brought more determination to read more difficult books, and by the end of the year Samantha was reading on a sixth-grade level. Samantha's desire to read increased each time she experienced success. She became more empowered to make decisions about her learning. As she became more empowered, her determination strengthened significantly. Each time following her success I could see her expectations rise. As her expectations rose, her desire to read increased incrementally. She was experiencing the Three D's of Success.

MAKING IT HAPPEN

Like most of the ideas in this book, using the Three D's of Success in a classroom requires teachers and students to make a perceptual shift. Regardless of how success oriented teachers or students might view themselves, focusing on the Three D's will increase the types and amounts of success in the classroom. Likewise, the fear of becoming addicted to failure will definitely decrease. How to make it happen? Every teacher will find a different way. We suggest the following strategy, based on research and our own lived experience:

- **Try the Three D's yourself.** If you plan to convince your students that the Three D's will help them find more success in their learning and in their lives, you will need to experiment with the model yourself. Identify one of your own goals—a goal that you want to achieve but one that has seemed impossible—and go through the Three D's. Choose a goal that you will be able to share with your students. Think about it. Imagine yourself achieving it. Decide to do what is necessary to achieve it. Talk about your decision with others. Then do it. Become determined. Once you have found some success (however small at first), see what happens to your expectations. As your expectations rise, note that your desire to do more increases. Keep working through the cycle until you experience each phase of the Three D's.

- **Share your experience with your students.** Once you have experienced the Three D's in helping you reach what seemed to be an unreachable goal, share your experience and a copy of the Three D's model with your class. You can use stories from read-aloud books or brief video clips from movies, such as *Hoosiers, Remember the Titans, Chariots of Fire,* or *Pride*. You might also consider stories of sports heroes or news articles depicting people who have succeeded where success seemed impossible. Before doing this, think of some class goals that you could set as a group—goals the class has never before reached. Ask students to come to consensus on one of those goals that they would like to achieve together. Help them see that if they want to achieve the goal, they will need to *desire it,* focus on it, and think about it, especially when they are not required to think about it. Encourage them to talk about the goal with each other to demonstrate that they have really *decided* to achieve it.

• **Develop a class plan for achieving the goal.** For students to become *determined,* they will need to develop and agree on a plan for achieving the hard-to-reach goal. You can do this with different levels of participation from the class members depending on their age and development. The more contribution they make, however, the greater will be their determination to achieve the goal. Enlist all students in the development of the plan. You can begin by asking for written suggestions that you combine and redistribute. The aim is to leave no one out of the process. Make certain that the plan includes natural, easy ways of tracking class members' progress. For example, in a math class, track the mean, median, and mode scores for each chapter assessment. Discuss with students the desired goal for each of these measures and show progress toward the goal on a chart viewed by all members of the class.

• **Implement the plan and track success.** To keep students working toward the goal, find successes, however small, every day and talk about those successes with the class. If you notice a day or two when the class seems to regress— moving away from the goal—avoid mentioning their poor performance. Rather, use the data to help you restructure your own teaching so that the next day can yield better performance. The key here is to find positive progress every day. This does not mean that you should manufacture good performance where none is to be found. The Three D's is not about pretending good things are happening when they're not. It is about focusing relentlessly and constantly on real success, even when the success comes in small increments.

• **Talk about the Three D's with individual students.** Build a culture of success in your classroom by talking about the Three D's with individual students, as well as with the whole class. For example, when a student who has been reluctant to focus on an assigned task finally exerts appropriate effort, you might say, "I can see you've really *decided* to do it. You've made a *decision* to succeed." Or when a student is working particularly hard to complete an assignment, you might say, "You seem really *determined*." Of particular importance, when a student is making obvious progress, you should reinforce that progress by saying, "It seems like you are *expecting* so much more of yourself than you did last week." The point is that the Three D's model is not something to be read and set aside. It's a way of teaching and learning. It needs to be built into the fabric of the class. When students begin using the terms *desire, decision, determination, success,* and *expectations* themselves, you will know that you are building a culture of success in the classroom.

2

Urgency
Not Pressure

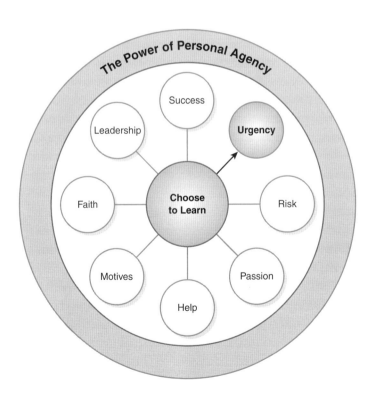

U rgency is an inner sense that propels someone to positive action. It is an impulse to move toward something good. A person, for example, might feel an urgency to help someone else in need. Brian Sturgill, a twenty-six-year-old man is such a person. While on a business trip, Brian was driving across the I-35W bridge in Minneapolis when the bridge collapsed and Brian's car fell sixty-five feet into the Mississippi River. Brian survived the fall, but his vehicle was partially submerged. Unable to open the door, he nearly panicked, but then he tried again and the door opened.

Once outside his vehicle, Brian saved the life of a man who was standing on top of his car with flames igniting all around him. Then, seeing two women who had no shoes, Brian went back to his car, broke open the window, popped his trunk, and retrieved shoes from his suitcase for the two women so they could make their way to safety. Attributing his heroism to a higher power, he concluded his interview, "Whenever there's a situation where you could've lost your life, it changes your perspective; it changes your outlook. All these things you take for granted, you come to appreciate a lot more" (Morales, 2007, p. 6).

Like Brian Sturgill, the most effective teachers develop a sense of urgency in themselves and in their students. Acting on that urgency can change one's perspective. This sense of urgency is part of what Schön (1983) calls "reflection in action." When teachers see a need, they do not have time to think about all possible solutions and to select the most appropriate. Rather, teachers develop an impulse to act intuitively and instantly to meet the immediate need. This is one of the defining differences between the expert and novice teacher (Johansson & Kroksmark, 2004; Westerman, 1990)—the ability to act in the moment to solve a problem a student presents, even when that problem is unexpected.

We are using the word *urgency* in a different way than many have used it. For example, for some the word *urgency* might convey negative emotions, such as becoming frantic, worried, or panicked. For others *urgency* refers to the timeliness of accomplishing a task. Covey (2004), for example, has described the relationship between *urgent* and *important,* suggesting that most people spend too much time on things that are urgent but not important, or even on things that are neither urgent nor important. A sense of urgency—the way we are using the term—implies both timeliness and importance but not worry or panic. An urgent goal is a worthy goal, one worth achieving. One cannot ignore the impulse to reach the goal anymore than Brian Sturgill could have sat idly by and watched others suffer.

Urgency, as we define it, goes even further. It also relies on faith—confidence that one can actually reach the worthy goal. There is an internal sense of confidence and peace that the path one is pursuing is the right path, the one that will lead to a successful conclusion. The combination of timeliness, importance, and faith propel the person to focus attention and effort on only one thing: reaching the worthy goal. Referring to the worthy goal of racial justice, Martin Luther King (1963) said, "We have come to this hallowed spot to remind America of *the fierce urgency of Now*" (p. 1; emphasis added).

Teachers must have a sense of urgency to teach effectively. Students must have a sense of urgency to learn effectively. Instilling urgency in students is a more important aim than presenting a few more facts to them. The more urgency students have, the more they will choose to learn and the less they will yield to distractions that compete for their attention. Students and teachers alike must feel the "fierce urgency of Now."

DIFFERENCES BETWEEN PRESSURE AND URGENCY

If urgency is the quality teachers want to foster in themselves and in their students, what should they avoid? For us, the most damaging impostor of urgency is *pressure.* Teachers feel pressure from so many sources. They can feel pressure from polices such as No Child Left Behind, from district mandates, from principals, from other teachers, from parents, or from students. The pressures may get so intense at times that teachers recoil, withdraw, or even leave the profession.

What's the difference between pressure and urgency? Table 2.1 shows the contrast between these two feelings.

Table 2.1   Desire, Urgency, and Pressure

	Urgency	*Pressure*
Desire: Think about it *now*	Welcome a challenge Yield to excitement Express gratitude	Avoid responsibility Succumb to discouragement Express resentment

Desire (Think About It *Now*)

Notice that the word *desire* in Table 2.1 comes from the first of the Three D's of Success model in the previous chapter. By contrasting characteristics of a person who has developed a sense of urgency with those who see themselves as always acting under pressure, one can easily see how urgency leads to the Three D's and how pressure leads to addiction. For example, a teacher who has a desire to succeed welcomes new challenges. One who allows desire to be influenced by outside pressure tends to avoid responsibility. A new challenge to this teacher is just one more unwanted duty, one more task for which there is no time. The two teachers might be in the same school, functioning with the same policies, and working with the same principal, but the teacher who has developed urgency is excited about her work, and the one who feels constant pressure succumbs to discouragement, loses desire, and stops innovating. The one with a sense of urgency also expresses gratitude much more frequently than the pressured teacher who often expresses resentment about the requirements of his profession.

Teachers who want their students to welcome new challenges, to be more excited about learning, and to express more gratitude for the privileges they've been afforded need to exemplify these qualities themselves. An unexcited teacher cannot excite anyone about learning. Students get excited about learning when they achieve a learning goal. Teachers who foster a sense of urgency in their students help students recognize their achievement, become excited about new possibilities, and convey that excitement to students.

When I was completing my master's degree, Lolly helped me conduct a study on preremedial instruction (Osguthorpe & Harrison, 1976). In that study, rather than identifying slower learners and then giving them remediation, we identified such learners and taught them a new concept that had not yet been introduced in their second-grade classroom. We chose the math concepts of carrying and borrowing. A pretest showed that even many of the fastest learners in the class did not yet understand these procedures. Tutors helped the slower learners master the concepts and then Lolly, acting as the classroom teacher, introduced the concepts to the entire class.

The results showed that the slowest learners performed significantly better on both carrying and borrowing than did the fastest learners. As the tables figuratively had been turned, the fastest learners were often perplexed as to how the slow learners were so proficient at something the faster learners did not know how to do. The slow learners clearly had more urgency about their learning because they had experienced success, and they knew they would experience more success as the teacher presented the concepts to the entire class.

Decision (Decide *Now*)

The choice between urgency or pressure impacts the way students and teachers make decisions. Table 2.2 shows these differences.

Entire books have been written on the role of intuition in the learning process (Noddings & Shore, 1999). Intuition is

Table 2.2   Decision, Urgency, and Pressure

	Urgency	*Pressure*
Decision: **Decide** *now*	Follow inner promptings Find reasons to succeed Focus on internal strengths	Ignore intuition and inspiration Find reasons to procrastinate Complain about outside requests

one way of making decisions. It's a process of looking inside oneself for answers. Inspiration is spoken of less frequently. One might say, "That was an inspired decision," meaning that the results of the decision have proven that it was a wise choice. Teachers and students who have a sense of urgency listen to the inner promptings that come in times of decision. When they're unsure, they move in the moment toward the goal they feel compelled to reach. Those who constantly feel pressure often ignore intuition and inspiration. They have difficulty receiving any type of prompting because their minds are always focused on outside inhibiting influences, and intuition and inspiration have been effectively blocked.

When deciding how to spend one's time or how to approach a new task, the person with urgency looks inside first. That person focuses on internal strengths and finds reasons to succeed. Those who function under pressure often find reasons to escape the task at hand, look forward to the end of the day or to retirement, and complain about unreasonable requests on their time. The chronic complainer is clearly addicted to failure.

Teachers need to help students overcome their tendency to complain and ask for exceptions to rules. Once, while supervising and training a group of more than one hundred young adults, we told them that we were thinking of creating an automatic phone answering system: "If you ask for an exception to a rule, press one." They press one: "Sorry, there are no exceptions." "If you have a complaint, press two." They press two: "Sorry, you must have the wrong number, we don't take complaints. We only take suggestions." We've also found this approach to be useful with students of any age in any setting who are prone to complain.

The point is that when teachers and students look outside themselves, feel pressured by demands that are made on them, and begin complaining, they become unproductive and even damaging to themselves and others. Teachers need to show students that complaining never helps. Constructive suggestions can move things forward, but never complaints.

An educator friend of ours, Beverly Cutler, shows how one person can reduce the frequency of complaining behavior in an entire organization. Anytime someone approaches Beverly with a complaint about the school, another teacher, or a student, Beverly's response is always the same. After listening to the complaint, she looks at the complainer with an "I've-understood-everything-you've-said" expression on her face and responds with two simple words: "I see." Her response communicates subtly to the complainer that she neither agrees nor disagrees but that she does not want to engage in the conversation further. She in essence turns off the complaining and shifts the conversation to a more productive topic.

Determination (Do It *Now*)

As Table 2.3 shows, the teacher or student who feels urgency reaches eagerly for the goal; the pressured person reluctantly complies with outside demands. Because such individuals comply reluctantly, they receive no benefit from their effort. The reluctant gift giver is not a giver at all. Unless one's heart is in it, even deeds that appear good on the surface are ultimately damaging to the one who holds back. Reluctance leads to addiction just as complaining does. Reluctance and complaining cannot lead to learning and improvement for either the teacher or the student.

Table 2.3   Determination, Urgency, and Pressure

	Urgency	*Pressure*
Determination: Do it *now*	Eagerly reach for goal Initiate new ideas Invite collaboration	Reluctantly comply with demands Wait for others' direction Reject offers of help

Urgency leads to initiation. Those who want to achieve a goal initiate ideas on their own. They don't wait to be told what to do. This is part of what is meant by Parker Palmer (1997) when he talks about "the courage to teach." Teaching and learning both require personal risk. Initiating new ideas is risky. The one who feels pressure loathes risk because the fear of failure overtakes the desire to succeed, and so, ironically, failure is assured.

Because those who feel urgency want to achieve the goal as soon as and as effectively as possible, they invite collaboration. They are not afraid of others who may be more competent in some area than they are. In fact, they are attracted to competence wherever they can find it. They want to succeed. So they welcome others' opinions. Those who feel pressure, contrarily, seek isolation. Because they don't want anyone telling them what to do, collaboration is at minimum a nuisance and can even be viewed as a form of failure. If success can occur only with others' help, the pressured person sees it as no success at all because the pressured person attributes the success to the one who helped.

Expectations (Expect More Success *Now)*

The person with urgency expects success. Table 2.4 shows the effects of this relationship.

Table 2.4   Expectations, Urgency, and Pressure

	Urgency	*Pressure*
Expectations: Expect more success *now*	Expect Success Expect help Expect constant improvement	Expect failure Expect roadblocks Expect things to get worse

As we explained in the previous chapter, these expectations continue to grow following each success. The pressured person, however, expects failure. Students addicted to failure know somewhere inside themselves that when they attempt a new task, they will fail. They have failed so many times in the past that they expect to fail again. Newness frustrates them and makes them feel even less adequate than they already feel. When students feel pressured, they perform far below their potential. When teachers feel pressured, they likewise fall short of what they are truly able to do.

Students and teachers who feel a sense of urgency expect to receive the help they need to achieve their goal. They invite others to assist them, but they also receive help at times when they least expect it. For example, I once had an English as a second language (ESL) student, Viviana, who would bring me her work and ask me several times a day, "Is this good?" or "Is this all right?" I resisted the urge to say something that would discourage her questioning because I sensed there was some unmet need. I kept encouraging Viviana by telling her that her daily writing was error free and had a strong voice. In fact her writing was every bit as good as any student's in the class. Then one day I was having a conversation in the hallway after school with the mother of one of Viviana's friends. We were discussing the progress of her own daughter when the mother mentioned the interactions she had had with Viviana's father.

When Viviana went over to play at her friend's house, Viviana was fearful of returning home even a few minutes late. Her father's unreasonable expectations sparked uneasiness in Viviana. There was no evidence of physical abuse, but there were issues of emotional control. It helped me to understand this child better, and I became eager to answer Viviana's questions and express my approval of her work. I loved every opportunity she afforded me to interact positively with her and accept her as a capable student.

Of all expectations for those who feel a sense of urgency, this perhaps is the most essential: to expect constant improvement. Because those who feel urgency have experienced success regularly, they come to expect themselves to do better, whereas those who feel pressure expect things to stay the same or get worse. They do not believe they can break out of the rut of failure because the ultimate cause of their failure is not them at all: it is due to outside forces over which they believe they have no control.

When I was in graduate school, I received a request to tutor a fourteen-year-old boy in reading. I agreed to be the tutor and began by administering a battery of reading tests. The results showed that although he was above average on intelligence tests and socially skilled, he could not even name all of the letters of the alphabet. Ron was in the ninth grade and had never read a book—any book—cover to cover. His mother was desperate to help him learn to read. She told me one day, "Oh, I think it's genetic. My husband has the same problem. He's severely dyslexic. He's a builder but always has to ask others to read the blueprints for him."

I had tried to help a number of other children improve their reading but never with as severe a deficit as Ron's. As we began he was reading on the preprimer level, but as the tutoring sessions progressed, he made visible progress. He had never mastered phonetic skills, and he latched onto every rule I could teach him. After several months of semiweekly tutoring, Ron was reading on the fourth-grade level and completed a book for the first time in his life. He later went to college, became an interpreter for the deaf, and continued to build on the foundation we had laid.

Ron's mother clearly felt a sense of urgency. She had tried other special programs before coming to us and had become frustrated, but Ron's continuing difficulties did not dissuade her. She was determined to help him, and she finally found a way to do it. Ron also felt urgency to learn how to read. One day he told me, "I've got to learn to read better because I'm the secretary in my scout troop, and I can't read everybody's name." His disability was beginning to take a toll on his relationships with others, and he wanted to improve. I also felt a sense of urgency, although I would never have used the term at the time I was tutoring Ron. His mother wanted him to succeed, I wanted him to succeed, and he wanted to succeed. There was urgency all around.

I suppose that I could have felt pressured by his mother and even by the professor who referred Ron to me, but I didn't. Ron could also have felt pressured by his mother or by his friends, but instead he seemed to have a deep-rooted desire to do better. If any of us had felt pressure, I believe the results would not have been as positive as they were. In fact, looking back now, I am persuaded that the programs Ron had tried before coming to me likely failed because the feeling of pressure took over and paralyzed everyone involved. Before I saw Ron, he had definitely become addicted to failure. He had failed so many times that he did not expect at first to succeed. Only after initial successes—very small successes—did he begin to develop a sense of urgency, and his successes fueled his mother's confidence and my faith that he could learn to read.

Urgency and Learning

I never observed Ron in a school classroom before he learned how to read, but I must assume that he was often not able to focus on the task at hand. Time was always passing, but Ron was likely thinking about something else, deciding something else, and doing something else. Like many students, his "time on task" was limited, and so he did not learn. All I really did was help him focus on the task long enough to experience some success. Then the success took over and caused his expectations to rise and his urgency to increase.

One of our favorite articles on time and learning was written by Benjamin Bloom (1974). In the article he describes numerous studies that show the difference between students' "elapsed time" and "time on task." He explains how the fastest students (as measured by aptitude and intelligence tests) in the class reach mastery of a new concept five times faster than the slowest students when simply measuring elapsed time, the time that passes when students are working on their own. What several researchers found was that the fastest students were more focused on the learning task, while the slowest students were sharpening pencils, talking to classmates, or doodling.

When students were helped to focus more on the learning task and work toward mastery, the fastest learners were still three times as fast as the slowest learners, but here is the clincher: When the slowest learners had experienced repeated success in mastering new concepts, the fastest learners were only one and a half times faster than the slowest learners. The more success students experienced, the less important intelligence and aptitude became in determining students' rate of learning. When they were not experiencing success, the slowest students felt little urgency to engage in the learning task, but as the successes multiplied, the urgency grew, their expectations for success increased, and they continually reached their goal. A colleague who chairs a department of mathematics encourages his faculty to say to students every day: "Remember, personal effort is more important than natural ability." He exhorts the faculty to convince students that even though they may not see themselves as mathematicians, they can still succeed if they exert themselves.

Lynn G. Robbins, former senior vice president of Franklin Quest Corporation, would probably say that the reason the slowest learners improved is because they could finally see their goal. He likens a goal to an island:

> Imagine for just a minute that you are out in the ocean lost and disoriented. You can't see land in any direction. How much motivation do you have to row? Somewhere between zero and none. Now changing the scenario: Out on the horizon you can see an island. *Now* how much motivation do you have to row? You not only have a lot more motivation to row, but you'll be rowing twice as hard and enjoying it more because now you have a vision, you have an island, you have a goal. The vision of the island is like adrenaline to the spirit to allow us to accomplish far more than we ever would if we didn't have the island (personal communication, June 24, 2004).

Bloom's (1974) slow learners found an "island" and then started to row faster and harder—and as Robbins explained—began to like it more. So their time on task changed dramatically, causing a marked increase in their rate of learning. Urgency took over because they could finally see the "island." The more teachers can help students see their goals, the more students will be eager to engage in the learning task, and the more eager they are, the more success they will experience.

MAKING IT HAPPEN

Like the Three D's, trading pressure for urgency is a personal endeavor. Helping students do the same is not done in a single lesson. We like to view urgency versus pressure as an overlay to the Three D's. So to make it happen in the classroom, you might consider the following:

 • **Examine your own life.** Just as with the Three D's, you can't teach urgency until you are experiencing it yourself.

Everyone feels urgency for something. The challenge is to feel urgency for what is required of us. We need to love what we have to do. So take a look at your own life. List the things that are required of you and then place the tables in this chapter next to your list. Do you have feelings of resentment or reluctance? Do you comply half-heartedly to demands placed upon you? Do you ever expect things to get worse? If you can find anything in the right column of the tables that describes your feelings of pressure, determine a plan to trade those feelings in and develop a sense of urgency. It is important to remember that people control their feelings; feelings don't control people.

• **Talk about urgency with the whole class.** Ask students to make a list of the things they feel pressure to do—things they feel they have to do but don't want to do. Then ask them to make a list of things they really want to do—things they wish they had more time to do. Help them see the difference between these two lists—that one represents pressure, and the other represents urgency. Ask them if they think they could change their feelings of pressure into urgency. Discuss how that might happen. Explain that they control their feelings; their feelings don't control them. Help them see the results of changing pressure into urgency—that they would experience more success in school and in life if they learn to love the things they have to do. Give examples from your own experience and from the experience of other successful people.

• **Teach with urgency.** When students see your excitement, they become excited. Talk about how important their success is to you. Celebrate their successes in ways that help them eliminate negative feelings of pressure and replace them with positive feelings of urgency. When you notice such a change, recognize it, so that students can see it for themselves. For example, some students become discouraged with a learning task and give up. They misplace their pencil, forget their notebook, and can't focus on the task at hand. They don't really want to try. When a student who has been discouraged about something shows any sign of excitement, say, "You're doing it because you really want to. I can tell you're not just doing it to get it done. You've got urgency."

- **Help students replace pressure with urgency.** When a student says, "I'm not really good at that," you can respond, "Oh, you feel pressure to do it, and you don't think you can? What if I proved to you that you could do it? Then you wouldn't feel pressure anymore, right?" When a student complains, say, "You're complaining because you feel pressured, right? So tell me how you can solve this, and then you will really want to do it, and you won't want to complain anymore." Your whole purpose here is to help students become aware of how they are acting out of pressure, how that leads to mediocre performance, and how replacing it with a feeling of urgency will lead to success.

"I want to but I don't think I can." When students express this dilemma, they might be saying, "I want to but I don't really want to." You might respond, "Are you afraid if you try, you might fail?" Student: "Yeah." Teacher: "But what have you got to lose? You know you can't improve unless you try, so let me show you how, and then you try." These simple, direct exchanges between teacher and student can help the student develop a sense of urgency and help eliminate feelings of pressure that lead to failure.

3

Do Something You've Never Done Before

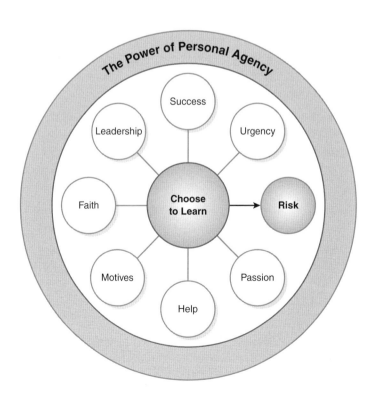

The Power of Personal Agency

Success
Leadership
Urgency
Faith
Choose to Learn
Risk
Motives
Passion
Help

Educators have struggled over the definition of the word *learning* for centuries. Some focus on the student as a creator of knowledge (Scardamalia & Bereiter, 2006). Others emphasize attitudinal change (Krathwohl, 1989). Still others point to permanent changes in behavior (Gagné, 1985). We like the following definition: "Doing something you've never done before." It's simple yet powerful. Yes, it emphasizes what the learner *does*, but the implications that lie beneath this act of *doing* are what matter most.

Doing something one has never done before demands courage—an attitudinal shift. It also requires knowledge. One cannot do something for the first time without some new knowledge aiding the process and even emerging during the process. Unlike others who have emphasized the importance of sustaining a newly learned skill, we assert that real learning comes as one builds on that skill. So learners are continually doing something they've never done before. It never stops.

While sitting on the tarmac preparing to fly home from Beijing, China, I saw the passenger behind me motion to the flight attendant for assistance. When the flight attendant approached the man and asked how she could help, the man pointed to the window of the airplane and demanded, "Please open this window, it's very stuffy in here." The flight attendant explained patiently that airplane windows do not open and offered to bring the passenger a drink of water. Those who overheard the conversation were amused by the request. It was obvious that this passenger was doing something he had never done before, and because the situation was completely new and unfamiliar, he was learning constantly.

Doing something one has never done before can occur in two primary ways: a person can attempt a totally new task, such as in the case of the airline passenger, or a person can perform substantially better a task that has been previously attempted. Let's take a look at college football, for example. All players are playing the same game, a game they have likely been playing for years, but some reach a level of mastery that far outstrips others. When asked how he felt about his team's receiving a preseason ranking of number one, Pete Carroll, the coach of the University of Southern California football team, responded: "That's what we're here for. We're here to do it better than anybody has ever done it before. That's the single thought. That's what drives us. If that's the case, you want to be No. 1 forever" (Russo, 2007, p. D9).

He did not say that he wanted his team to improve upon the previous season or that he was hoping for a better performance from his quarterback than last year. He said that he wanted his team to perform better than any team had ever performed—to play the same game but to play it better than it has ever been played: doing something that has never been done before.

In keeping with the Three D's, he alluded to desire ("You *want* to be No. 1"), decision ("That's what we're here for"— that's what we've decided to do), and determination ("That's what drives us"). Some might conclude that a coach's goals are too heavily oriented toward competition, a feeling that should not be the motivating force for learners in a classroom, but we argue that his statement focuses on a standard more than on the performance of competitors. The team wants to become so proficient that competitors cannot even come close to matching their performance. They want to do something better than it has ever been done before. That means that each player needs to reach a level of excellence that he has never previously reached. So the ultimate competition is not with other players (or with other learners in a classroom): it is competition with one's own past performance.

WHY AVOID THE UNFAMILIAR?

Rather than avoiding new tasks, students and teachers need to embrace the unexpected, the new, the unfamiliar. By *embrace* we mean that students and teachers need to do more than tolerate something they have never before experienced, they need to wrap their minds around it, become acquainted with it, and, yes, enjoy it. That is when real learning occurs. When one embraces the unfamiliar, that unfamiliar thing enters the person's life and becomes familiar, much like a kind stranger knocking on our door—a stranger who wants to give us a gift that will help meet one of our personal needs. We permit the stranger to enter, we sense the person's sincerity, and we come to know the person. As the person prepares to depart, we embrace because the stranger is no longer unfamiliar but has become a friend.

Unfortunately, avoiding the unfamiliar is probably more common in human experience than embracing it. Why do so many avoid experiences that seem foreign? We suggest that the primary reason is fear. In the case of learning and teaching, it is a specific kind of fear—the fear of failing. A student avoids completing an algebra assignment because "math is hard." A teacher avoids experimenting with a new way of teaching reading because, "I don't have time to learn a new program." The word *fear* appears in neither the student's nor the teacher's comments, but it is the ultimate cause of refusing to try new ways of doing things.

We worked once with a teenage student who was failing at nearly everything he attempted. We could see that fear was keeping him from trying to succeed. We asked, "So are you afraid that if you try, things could get worse?" He nodded in the affirmative. "Well," we continued, "things are already worse; they can't get any worse. What do you really have to lose by trying?" He was addicted to nonperformance, convinced that doing nothing—that never trying to improve—was more appealing than taking a risk and failing. His thinking was a little bit like the college student who decides to aim for a C grade, because then there will be no disappointment. If the student aims for an A and then gets a C, the learning experience will be frustrating, or so the student reasons. So why not just go for the C?

THE ZONE OF ATTAINABLE SUCCESS

Doing something one has never done before involves risk. Students, such as the one just described, who do nothing because they fear that things could get worse, or students who aim for a C, are taking no risk at all. Rather than "keeping the light on just in case a stranger might come," they keep their door closed and locked with a deadbolt. No risk. No challenge. No progress.

Taking manageable risks for the learner is much like a teacher finding the "zone" within which a student is stretched but can succeed. Vygotsky coined the phrase "zone of proximal development." As Hedegaard (2005, p. 228) explained Vygotsky's theory, "The main characteristic of instruction is that it creates a 'zone of proximal development' stimulating a series of inner developmental processes." Unlike Piaget, who believed that instruction was incidental to development, Vygotsky believed that instruction stimulated the child's development (Newman & Newman, 2005), but both Piaget and Vygotsky focused more on human development than on the power of planned instruction to help the learner progress.

We believe that teachers and learners alike need to focus on a *zone of attainable success*. We have already defined success as going beyond previous achievement—doing something you've never done before. So the zone we believe teachers and students need to focus on is one in which the learner is challenged to stretch beyond any previously achieved goal to achieve a new level of success. This means taking manageable risks—both for the teacher and for the learner. The teacher may not be certain that the student can succeed at a given task, so the teacher asks the student to attempt it. During the attempt, the teacher may adjust the task by making it more difficult or easier depending on the needs of the learner, but the whole focus is on success—doing better or doing more than the student has done before.

Those who design video games understand well what we are calling the zone of attainable success. Anyone who has watched a child or youth play a video game quickly concludes that games are more engaging than most instruction that takes place in schools. Why are games so engaging? Because the player is constantly challenged to do something new, to "move to the next level." The game designers understand well the notion of zone of attainable success. If the game is too easy, it bores the player. If it's too hard, the player gives up—finds another game. It is the relentless constancy of challenge that keeps the player engaged.

Some educators have concluded that more classroom instruction needs to take the form of games. Richard Swan (2008) argues that such efforts have not been very successful as stimulants to student motivation in schools. The games that find their way into school computer labs are either not as motivating as real video games, not instructionally effective, or last such a short time that the student is soon back in the classroom with instruction that is not very engaging. The solution, as Swan (2008) suggests, is to help teachers develop learning activities that take advantage of the design features of games without actually *being* games.

For example, I asked my class to use the online dictionary on their computers to look up vocabulary words for definitions and parts of speech. Students worked in pairs and accomplished the learning task in record time. We recorded the time required for everyone to finish and then tried to beat our time each week. Attention to the task increased dramatically as the class became more efficient and focused. Everyone succeeded at a task that for some students is difficult even to start without a great deal of prodding and help.

TEACHER AS DESIGNER

Teachers typically do not see themselves as instructional designers. They often view themselves more as consumers of instructional products developed by others, but teachers are designing every day. They are determining how existing materials will be used, how new tasks will be presented, and how students will demonstrate mastery. In one sense, a teacher's primary role is to *design* the environment in which students can thrive—to design ways to help students take risks, to stretch themselves, to try new things, to do something they've never done before.

When a teacher creates a new way of helping students learn, the teacher is engaging in the process of design. The process often leads to the development of tools or aids for learning. For example, a teacher might develop a new type of math manipulative to teach students about decimals. Design can also lead to the development of a new learning strategy, such as teaching spelling rules using songs.

Browsing a publication, I noticed an article about a teacher in California who had developed songs to teach math, spelling, and grammar rules to his third graders (Bedley, 2007). Having used songs and rap before to teach prepositions and helping verbs, I was intrigued and went to his Web site. He had a CD for sale with the songs recorded by his kids, but he also provided a printable version of the words to his songs. After printing the words on chart paper for the students, I accompanied the class with my ukulele as we sang about parts of speech and four kinds of sentences. I find that these songs are a great way to introduce a topic and an easy way for repetition to take place without boring my students. On another day we made a movie clip of our class singing the songs for our class Web site. Then we learned basic chords on the ukuleles I found stashed in the back of a school storage closet and kept rehearsing our songs. Music is a powerful tool to help students remember facts.

Design, such as Bedley's (2007) song mnemonics, can lead to any new product or strategy. Architects design buildings. Electrical engineers design cell phones and computers. Effective design improves our lives. It can improve the lives of teachers and students. As Nelson and Stolterman (2003) explain the power of design:

We are pulled into design because it allows us to initiate intentional action out of strength, hope, passion, desire, and love. It is action which generates more energy than it consumes. It is innovative inquiry that creates more resources—of greater variety and potential—than are used. Design action is distinct from problem action, which is initiated out of need, fear, weakness, hate, pain, and other reactive motivations. (p. 17)

These authors are implying that teachers can be attracted to design because design permits the teacher to try something new—to take risks, to question how students can learn more effectively. In this way, design is to the teacher as learning is to the student—flip sides of the same coin. Our premise is that the more the teacher tries new ways of helping students learn, the more likely the students will be to take similar risks in their learning—to stretch beyond past achievements. We like the notion of Nelson and Stolterman (2003) that design— and we are using the term in its broadest sense—"creates more energy than it consumes and more resources than are used." A successful learning activity—one that engages the learner—may take some "design" time for the teacher (some energy and resources), but it leads to more energy, more effort, more concentration, and more learning on the part of the student than the teacher consumes in its production.

Every time a teacher thinks of a strategy to help students master a certain task, the teacher should think of the energy the student will be expending. What will students be *doing?* How will students prove to themselves and to the teacher that they have mastered this new task? When teachers create effective learning activities, they are fueling the energy level of students. Effective strategies are adopted by other teachers, and the energy expended just keeps expanding. So teachers need to constantly be drawn in by the power of design to effect learning, to help students experience more success. Then teachers will be doing things they've never done before, just as they are asking students to do things they've never done before.

Thus the student is stretching to achieve a new task in the zone of attainable success, and the teacher is creating a learning environment that challenges the student to reach a little higher and do a little better. This act of creating and designing can have the same effect on the teacher as the challenging learning activity has on the student. It renews. It lifts. It energizes. If teachers could see their role in this way, there would be less burnout. If students could respond likewise, there would be more success and less failure in the classroom. Success lifts the learner, the teacher, the classmate, the parent, the administrator—everyone. For this reason, when the student and the teacher both *choose to learn,* everyone benefits because everyone succeeds.

MAKING IT HAPPEN

This is actually a very enjoyable principle to implement in your class, because it applies in so many situations. Your goal is to help students relish the challenge of doing new things for the first time or doing familiar things better than they have ever done them before. Here are some specific suggestions:

• **Develop a new talent.** Sometimes adults forget what it feels like to do new things. If you plan to help students get excited about newness, you will need to experience it along with them. One of the best ways to do this is to develop a new talent. Choose something that has always interested you but that you've never had time to develop. It might be in the visual arts, music, dance, sports, fitness, cooking—whatever you choose. Then sign up for lessons or get a coach or trainer or just get a book and learn it on your own, but choose a talent and develop it.

• **Talk about talents with your class.** Share your own experience developing a new talent and explain how each student could do the same. Discuss the talents that students are now developing and ask them to share how they felt when they made real progress—when they did something they'd never done before. Liken talent development to academic learning and discuss how those same feelings of accomplishment come when we achieve a new level of academic excellence in any school subject.

- **Emphasize the process of discovery.** Whatever content you are teaching, first identify well-known experts in the field, those who have made important discoveries. In history, you could cite early explorers and ask students what it felt like to discover some new mountain or lake. If you're teaching science, you can point to some great scientific discoveries and ask students to imagine how that felt to achieve such a discovery. For art, you can talk about how a new art form or style is developed and how the artist who introduced that art form or style may have felt as it was developed. These are examples of doing something that no one has ever done before. Next, show how good it feels to do something for the first time yourself, even if others have already done it—for example, swimming across the pool, playing a song on the guitar, or writing a convincing essay for the first time. Then discuss with the class how you plan to emphasize this type of learning—looking for things they've never done before and earnestly seeking to do them. Ask them how they think this will help them feel a sense of urgency, as discussed in the last chapter, and how it will motivate them to succeed.

- **Encourage the whole class to do what they have never done before.** Help the class achieve a goal that no class before them has ever achieved. You might use examples from your own experience to show how some classes exceeded the performance of any other previous class. Jaime Escalante's story, as depicted in the movie *Stand and Deliver*, of helping students succeed on the calculus advanced placement exam is one possible example. You might show clips from films of such stories and discuss how these examples could apply to your class.

- **Use key indicators to track student learning.** Identify as a class the most important measurable learning goals that you are seeking to achieve, such as test performance, number of minutes students read outside of class, homework packets completed, and amount of socially appropriate behavior during the school day. Ask students to keep track of their own performance on each key indicator. Then summarize the performance for the entire class and show how the class is making progress toward the desired goal. The important aspect of key indicators is that students become acutely aware of how well they are doing so that they can stretch to do better—to do something they've never done before—just as players in a game move from a lower level to a higher level. Remember to identify only the most important key indicators, keeping the number to a bare minimum. You can change the key indicators periodically to meet the students' needs. Track only the performance that you can easily measure, then display the results of the key indicators for the entire class, and use the results to motivate students to do even better.

• **Do something new every day.** You cannot expect students to be experimental and try new things unless you are setting the example for them in your own pedagogy. It might sound unrealistic to do something new every single day, but it is possible, and it may even be essential to avoid burnout. The new teaching method might be something as simple as providing feedback to an individual student in a new way. It might be a whole new learning activity for the entire class that you've never tried before. For example, you might organize cooperative learning groups in a new way by designating a student leader for each group to keep track of the group's key indicators. You might design new seating arrangements that promote more effective collaboration among students. You might identify the hurdles or trouble spots in a particular lesson and design a new strategy for helping students overcome the common misconceptions that interfere with their learning. You could ask students to indicate with a simple thumbs-up or thumbs-down whether they are ready to proceed further in a lesson, or if they need more explanation. The point is to commit to yourself to try something new every day, and when you try it, explain to students that you are doing it so that you can see if it works—you're trying to improve, just as you expect them to improve, by trying new things.

• **Chart class progress.** People are motivated by seeing and acknowledging the progress they are making. Sometimes progress is so imperceptible by individuals that they don't recognize improvement when it actually happens. Once you begin to encourage students to do things they've never done before, you can chart their progress and refer to the chart often to show them how much progress they are making. For example, you might use a chart that shows the mean performance of the class on writing, spelling, math, science— whatever you want to track and improve. You explain to students that you are expecting classwide improvement on the topic you are charting. Each time you measure their performance, you ask a student to update the chart. It can be a chart done in PowerPoint, a written chart on the wall, or a three-dimensional thermometer the students create— whatever you choose to help students see that the whole class can keep improving by doing things they've never done before.

• **Identify individual goals.** Regularly invite students to write down something that they have never done before but that they want to accomplish in school. A bulletin board with a library pocket for each student holding 3 × 5 cards with recorded goals works well. The goals could also be written in each student's journal. A weekly individual goal could be taped on a young child's desk as a daily reminder. Follow up each week to encourage the students to reach their goals.

4

Light the Fire

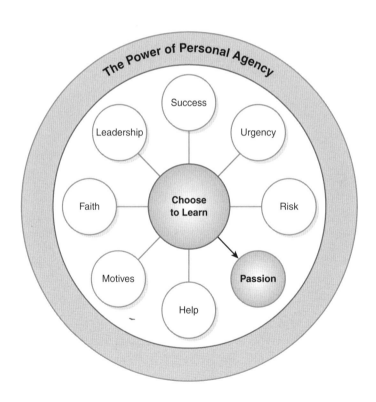

When our grandchild Molly was two years old, she was very intent on learning how to buckle herself into her booster chair. We captured her "learning" on video. The video begins with Molly trying to climb up into the chair without any help from the family members watching her. When she succeeds in sitting in the chair, she grabs the two ends of the safety belt and begins to orient each side of the buckle so that it will snap together. Watching closely we all give encouragement, telling her that she can do it. She finally gets the sides of the buckles lined up, inserts the one side into the other, but it doesn't quite go. We keep giving encouragement but never touch the buckle. "Kinda hard," she says, and we echo: "Yes, it's kinda hard! But you can do it." And she keeps trying. Pushing with all her might, the buckle comes together and locks. Screaming at the top of her lungs, Molly exults, "I did it!" And then she keeps repeating it again and again: "I did it! I did it!"

Molly's example is what most teachers and students wish learning were like all the time. No one is forcing Molly to learn. She's self-motivated and self-directed. No one is asking her to take a test following the learning experience. Assessment is built into the activity itself. She knows, as does everyone who is standing around her, that she has succeeded. The task itself was the test, and she passed it. Because it was something she had never done before, she was especially excited about achieving her goal. It was challenging, but it was also attainable. Once she mastered the buckle, she was ready to get down out of the chair and go try another learning task. Her success led to increased expectations and an increased desire to tackle something new.

William Butler Yeats once said, "Education is not the filling of a pail, but the lighting of a fire" (see Evenbeck & Hamilton, 2006). He was restating a much older saying by Socrates: "Education is the kindling of a flame, not the filling of a vessel." So if this thought has been around for so long, why do so many educators see their purpose as filling a pail or bucket—putting facts in students' heads that students can later restate on a test? It happens in K–12 education as well as in postsecondary learning. Education is erroneously viewed as the total amount of information a person has acquired rather than the intensity of a person's desire to learn more.

We firmly believe that one reason some students become addicted to failure in formal schooling is because the system focuses so heavily on force-feeding information to learners rather than motivating them to search for it themselves. If education were focused on lighting fires rather than filling buckets, much in the processes of teaching and learning would change, and the changes would benefit both student and teacher. What would education look like if it were aimed at lighting a fire in the learner and teacher? What do teachers think about when they create a learning experience for students? They ask themselves three primary questions:

1. What do I expect students to know and be able to do following the learning experience?

2. How will I help them achieve mastery of the outcomes?

3. How will I measure their level of mastery?

To light a fire in both the learner and the teacher, all three of these questions need to be addressed. Table 4.1 shows the beginning of a framework that is built around the three main elements of any learning experience.

But students don't think much about these elements. Something else in the learning equation matters more to them: human relationships. Most learners don't consciously recognize the centrality of relationships to their learning, but when they are asked to rank the factors that contribute to their success—to their ability to light their own fire—the most common responses focus on the relationship that develops between

Table 4.1   Light the Fire: Three Main Elements

Learning Outcomes	Learning Activities	Learning Assessments

student and teacher (Baker, 1999; Benard, 1995; Feldman, 1988; Muller, 2001). So our framework for lighting a fire rests on a foundation of caring relationships. As seen in Table 4.2, we call them *edifying* relationships (Osguthorpe, 1997).

Table 4.2   Light the Fire: Edifying Relationships

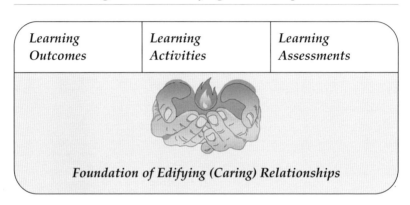

Learning Outcomes	Learning Activities	Learning Assessments
Foundation of Edifying (Caring) Relationships		

Why do we say "edifying" relationships? To edify is to build up. In French it literally means to construct a building. It is, however, a uniquely powerful kind of building; edification is a strengthening of the whole person, a movement toward virtue, a literal building up of the soul of both the learner and the teacher. This is the type of relationship that teachers and students long for. It is the type of relationship that is essential if the teacher and student are to light a fire for learning and keep it burning.

Linked to the Life of the Learner

Table 4.3 clarifies how teachers need to give careful thought to how each of the three stages should be linked to the life of the learner.

Learning how to buckle a belt on a booster seat was clearly linked to Molly's life as a two-year-old. The seat itself was a very important part of her daily life. She needed to get buckled

Table 4.3   Light the Fire: Linked

	Learning Outcomes	*Learning Activities*	*Learning Assessments*
Linked	Outcomes, activities, and assessments are *linked* to each other and to the life of the learner.		
	Foundation of Edifying (Caring) Relationships		

into it multiple times every day if she wanted to eat. Her mother did not need to tell her that learning how to buckle the belt was linked to her life: Molly already understood that, but with older learners, the tie between the learning outcome and the life of the learner becomes so loose that often the teacher cannot articulate it. A colleague recently explained: "When I took calculus in high school, I asked the teacher why we were learning it—what it was used for—and the teacher responded, 'Everyone should learn calculus.' He really couldn't give me an answer at all" (Paul F. Merrill, personal communication, September 18, 2007).

I responded with an experience I had at the university as a participant in an experimental calculus course taught to faculty—something I'd never done before. During the course an engineering professor showed a video of one Honda Accord crashing into the driver-side door of another Honda Accord. He showed how, without calculus, we could not predict the effect of the crash on either the passenger or the driver, but, with calculus, we could show that the force of the crash would kill the driver, who absorbed the major impact of the crash, and that the passenger would be relatively unharmed. Soon after that dramatic portrayal of mathematics, a friend of mine was killed in a crash nearly identical to the one depicted in the video the engineering professor had shown us. My friend's wife, who was the passenger in the car, had some bruises but was able to greet everyone at her husband's funeral. Calculus was not a set of formulas and abstract numbers. It was as real a concept to me as buckling that belt was for Molly. It was *linked* to my life.

Teachers at all levels need to consciously focus on linking learning outcomes, learning activities, and assessments to the life of the learner. We like teachers to think of it this way: convince students that they cannot live without learning what you are trying to teach them. In short, "You cannot live without this." For young children, this is not a difficult task. Learning to walk, to talk, to eat, to dress themselves—these are all naturally a part of their life—learning outcomes they are focusing on every day. But as the child grows older, the linkage between the learner's life and the task at hand becomes more abstract. Helping eighth graders understand why they cannot live without learning algebra is a different challenge than helping a one-year-old understand why she needs to learn how to drink from a cup.

Even if the outcomes and activities are linked to the life of the learner, the assessments may still be detached and artificial. If, however, the teacher attempts to tie the assessment methods to the life of the learner, the students begin to see assessment in a whole different way. The assessments become ways of demonstrating mastery rather than a means of obtaining a grade. Imagine, for example, a science teacher who tells students that they need to learn about bacteria so that they can pass the state core exams at the end of the year, versus the science teacher who convinces students that learning about bacteria could save their life. In the tradition of filling a bucket, the first teacher asks students to read the chapter, take a quiz, and then study for the exam. The second teacher asks students to identify bacterial infections that they and their friends or family members have experienced and to identify those that could be life threatening.

Students of the second teacher come back to class and describe staff infections, gastrointestinal infections, "flesh-eating" bacterial infections, and so on. They are amazed at the number and variety of bacteria that affect their life and the lives of their acquaintances. They ask questions about the origins of different bacteria and the ways of controlling bacterial infections with antibiotics. Students in the filling-the-bucket class ask questions about what will be on the next quiz and how much the quiz will count on their grade. In essence, the students in the first group are asking the teacher, "So just how full do I need to fill the bucket in order to get a passable grade?" while the lighting-the-fire group are asking questions that lead to more learning—all because the outcomes, activities, and assessments have been linked directly to their life.

CHALLENGING

Not only must outcomes, activities, and assessments be linked to the life of the learner, but also they must be challenging if a fire is to be lit (see Table 4.4). As explained in the previous chapter, outcomes that light a fire in the learner are new experiences for the student, things they've never done before. They are also *worthy* of the teacher's and learner's time. Curriculum in public schooling is not the invention of an individual teacher, principal, parent, or legislator. It is the expression of the society as a whole. If state core tests emphasize reading, writing, and arithmetic, it is because most in the society believe that these are skills that schools should impart to students.

So if the ultimate outcomes of formal schooling are predetermined, inviolate decisions of the culture in which we live, what freedom does a teacher have to craft outcomes in ways that light a fire in the learner? Actually, more freedom than one might think. A teacher can either feel restricted and confined by state core curriculum, or—and this requires a leap of faith—a teacher can feel freed by these goals imposed by society. They can be viewed as cords that tie us down as

Table 4.4   Light the Fire: Challenging

	Learning Outcomes	*Learning Activities*	*Learning Assessments*
Linked	Outcomes, activities, and assessments are *linked* to each other and to the life of the learner.		
Challenging	Outcomes, activities, and assessments are *challenging* yet attainable.		

Foundation of Edifying (Caring) Relationships

educators or "bonds that make us free," commitments with the power to ultimately liberate us (see Warner, 2001).

How can state goals free teachers? By offering them a challenge to make the pathway to the state goals irresistible for the students. Most teachers would agree that the overall goals society has for its children and youth are worthy of attainment, but the challenge for the teacher is to create activities and assessments that lead to those goals in ways that will light the fire in every learner.

One elementary teacher, Karre Neverez, designed her science curriculum around a fictitious crime scene that paralleled their literature study of *The Westing Game*, a Newbery Medal winner detailing a similar set of events (Hancock, 2007). Using materials such as iodine, instant adhesive, liquid putty, and pH testing kits, Neverez used the crime scene scenario to spark her students' science interest and to teach the scientific method. We know it takes hours to execute projects like this, but is there any doubt that her students have increased their understanding of analyzing, comparing, and interpreting evidence? One creative activity like Neverez's may be worth more than a year of lessons covering the curriculum to pass the end-of-level tests.

That leads us from outcomes to activities. Each activity has its own aim that helps students achieve the ultimate outcome in that domain. As explained in the previous chapter, learning activities need to be in the zone of attainable success. The definition of success is "doing better than you think you can do," or "doing something you once thought impossible." This definition of success points to the aspect of challenge in each activity. If the learner has achieved the task before, it's not challenging, or if the student feels no enticement to learn the task, it is still not challenging. If the activity is challenging, it draws the student in, pulls on the student's previous accomplishments, and beckons the student to "climb the next ridge."

Jeremy, a sixth-grade student, showed what can happen when a learning activity is challenging yet attainable. Jeremy spent half of his day in special education classes trying to boost his reading and math scores. Barely reading on a second-grade level, he seemed withdrawn and confused when in my regular class.

While teaching a social studies unit, I asked my students to choose or design a project about Egypt to share with our class as a culminating activity. I told my students to choose something that really interested them and that inspired them to be an expert teacher. They were to prepare to teach the class all that they had learned and to teach the class without reading their report.

Every day I reminded my students about their upcoming project and that this project would tell me if they had learned anything about Egypt. Jeremy would come to me after school and clarify details and dates to make sure that he would be prepared on the right day. Not only was he prepared, but Jeremy completed *two* projects. He taught our class well, explaining in detail everything he had learned and exhibiting some special artistic talent that drew praise from other students.

But the most amazing by-product of all this was that he listened intently to each report and asked a meaningful question of each student—behaviors that I had not previously witnessed in him. He was fascinated with ancient Egypt and clearly yearned to know more.

After all the project presentations, I asked the students to give themselves the grade they thought they deserved. Jeremy came to me unsure of what to do. I said, "Jeremy, did you try your very best? Did you do some things that you've never done before? In your heart, what do you think you deserve?" He smiled at me and understood for perhaps the first time that he too could succeed.

Jeremy's example shows that challenge is an important aspect of any learning activity. He was so drawn to the challenge that he exceeded the expected requirements of the assignment: Jeremy was enticed to master the topic of the assignment. The "test" in this case was an oral report and project, and he was so challenged that he did twice as much as he had been asked to do.

INSPIRING

Table 4.5 shows the third characteristic for lighting a fire in the student and in the teacher.

Inspiration leads to discovery. It is a process of being irresistibly enticed to acquire new knowledge. When a learning experience is inspiring, it takes on a life of its own in the student and in the teacher. The student cannot stop seeking until an answer is found, and the teacher cannot stop searching for better ways to help students learn. Both are drawn together to reach for the "highest in them," as one author has defined it (Madsen, 1978).

What is the "highest in us"? It is more than mastering a new learning task. It is more than simply meeting another challenge. It is a yearning for something that we know we were meant to do, but each time we approach the desired goal, it seems to slip further from our grasp. The more we

Table 4.5   Light the Fire: Inspiring

	Learning Outcomes	*Learning Activities*	*Learning Assessments*
Linked	Outcomes, activities, and assessments are *linked* to each other and to the life of the learner.		
Challenging	Outcomes, activities, and assessments are *challenging* yet attainable.		
Inspiring	Outcomes, activities, and assessments *inspire* students and teachers to reach for the "highest in them."		

Foundation of Edifying (Caring) Relationships

learn, the more we recognize our inadequacy. The more knowledge we acquire, the more our lack of knowledge haunts us. So we keep reaching for the highest in us, but only if the fire for learning is burning inside. This is the role of inspiration in our learning. It pulls us, draws us, ever upward, ever closer to the truth that so often eludes us.

Learning experiences that are linked, challenging, inspiring: that's what teachers need to do to light a fire in students and to keep the fire burning bright in themselves. Teachers can use the framework shown in Table 4.5 as a tool as they reflect on each of the three main elements of their instruction. They can ask if their learning outcomes are linked, challenging, and inspiring, whether their learning activities have those characteristics, and whether their assessment techniques meet those criteria. Perhaps most important of all, they can reflect on the relationship they have forged with each student and ask themselves if it is an edifying one—if both the student and teacher are "built up" by it, or if one or both is being diminished in some way.

There is a teacher somewhere, right now, educating a young learner who will one day win a Nobel Prize. This teacher and student are both choosing to learn. They are both building up each other. They are thinking of education not as filling a bucket but as lighting a fire. They both refuse to become addicted to failure. What are Nobel Prize winners like?

Let's look at a recent winner of the prize in medicine. Three distinguished scientists, Mario Capecchi, Oliver Smithies, and Sir Martin Evans won the 2007 Nobel Prize in medicine (see Collins, 2007). They discovered how to disable genes—a contribution that most thought was impossible. They were simply trying to *learn* how to do something that no one had ever done before. Capecchi obviously had a fire burning inside that fueled his learning. When other scientists tried and failed, he seemed more determined than ever. It was something he felt he was meant to do. When he applied for a National Institutes of Health grant, they told him that they felt his goal was impossible. Then, when he began to find his first success, they were eager to give him more funding. He expected to succeed, and he did.

The challenge of those who said it was impossible only strengthened his resolve. Without a little inspiration, he likely would never have made his groundbreaking discovery. Each new bit of learning strengthened him so he could climb the next peak. His learning not only resulted in his own discoveries but undoubtedly helped light a fire in those who worked with him. His inspiration inspired others. This is the message of this chapter: Every time a teacher is fanning her own flame of learning, the flames of those she teaches will increase. Thoughts of failure will fade. Expectations for success will grow, and students and teachers alike will achieve the highest in them.

MAKING IT HAPPEN

• **Teach the topic with passion.** Students often say, "It's a lot easier for me to get excited about learning if the teacher's excited." Neither teachers nor students can manufacture excitement. It must come naturally. So each time you teach a topic, find the aspect of the topic that excites you personally and then convey that to students. This often happens when you link it to your own life. Then you can link it more easily to the life of the learner. Show excitement for the topic by showing how you have "not been able to live without it." When a student asks, "So why do we need to know how to do percents?" You could say to the student:

> I have to know how to use percents every time I go shopping or when I go out to eat. If you go on a date someday, you've got to know how much to tip the server. That means you need to know how to multiply 15 percent or 20 percent times the cost of your meal. Or if you want to buy a new shirt at the store, you need to be able to estimate quickly what "20 percent off" means. You really can't live without knowing how to do percents.

• **Make learning outcomes exciting.** Old-time learning objectives can be less than exciting for both students and teachers, but you can make your learning outcomes exciting. For example, rather than saying, "Our goal by the end of the year is to meet the minimal benchmarks on math and reading," you could say, "Our goal by the end of the year is to do better than our class has ever done before on the state core tests in math and reading." A small, but potentially important, change in an outcome like this can light the fire for students.

• **Link everything to the life of the learner.** Challenge students to use what they learn in their everyday life. Ask for reports on how they are using what they're learning. If they're working on their writing skills, how are they using writing in their everyday lives? Make assignments that help them see how writing can be used at any age. They might write a letter to the editor, a proposal to the school principal, an e-mail to a relative—any assignment that gets them writing in their real life. Keep samples of their out-of-class writing. Compare samples. Use the comparisons to teach as well as to assess progress. Have them keep these samples in a portfolio so they can look back and measure their own improvement. Explain to them how these real-life assessments are like tests, even though they did not think of them as tests. Discuss with them how they will experience these kinds of real-life assessments throughout their life when they become employed.

• **Express confidence in students.** When students talk about teachers who helped light a fire for learning, they usually point to a teacher who expressed confidence in them. We are not talking here of random praise. We are suggesting that you express genuine confidence in students' potential to go far beyond the level at which they are now performing. A student, for example, gets 100 percent on a math test. Instead of simply praising the student—for example, "You've achieved your goal, excellent work!"—you say, "I've been watching you during math class, and you know what? You have a lot of talent in math. You could do anything you want in this field." When you express this kind of confidence, you point the student toward the future. You recognize the present success but only for the purpose of building the student so that greater accomplishments can be realized in the future. Expressing this kind of confidence in someone edifies the learner.

• **Relate to the difficult student.** Most teachers struggle from time to time with a student who is less than engaged, less than socially capable. Rather than ignoring this student, find ways to connect. When the student needs correction, give it, but give it with a boost of positive encouragement. For example, Mark, a behavior- and learning-challenged student, later diagnosed with mild autism, started the school year in my class with multiple instances of fighting on the playground. As his record had preceded him, I was gritting my teeth, but I decided that I would expect more. I noticed that Mark loved football. He was in my homeroom class and finished his work quickly, but he didn't understand the content, and his scores were very low. At first he would sulk if I offered correction and refuse my help. Positive interactions were few and far between. After multiple attempts, with the help of the school advocate, we designed a program that required Mark to look me in the eye, willingly accept help if needed, and be trouble free on the playground for a month. In return, the school advocate offered to arrange for a football player from the university to come and visit with Mark if he maintained his part of the bargain. In our class I offered a prize to the student who correctly guessed the weekly football score, and Mark, being an avid fan, frequently was the winner. There were a few minor setbacks, but we all persisted, and finally the day arrived when Mark's favorite player came with two other star players on the team. It was a day of triumph for a young student who previously had been addicted to failure.

5

Help Is
on the Way

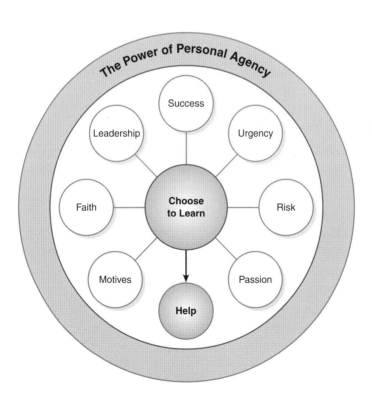

In the last chapter we asserted that somewhere right now a teacher is teaching a future Nobel Prize winner. That same teacher might also have a student with a serious disability, such as Down syndrome. The future Nobel Prize winners need help to reach the highest in them, but so do those with disabilities. The help given to one hardly resembles the help needed by the other. The ultimate success of both the teacher and the student rests on the teacher's ability to provide the right kind of help to each learner at the right time. In an educational setting focused on success, learners and teachers alike need to know that when they need help, help is on the way.

We believe that there are three primary types of help—some of which are not often thought of as such by teachers or students: (a) help that invites, (b) help that instructs, and (c) help that confirms. The second of the three is what most teachers think of when they provide help to their students—instructional assistance. It is what occupies their minds and takes the greatest amount of time in the school day, but it is not the only kind of help students need, and it may not even be the most important in the end.

HELP THAT INVITES

Some educational theorists have structured everything around the "invitation" (Purkey, 2000, 2002). It might be called invitational learning, invitational education, or invitational leadership. We are not promoting this particular approach to education. We are, rather, suggesting that invitation is an essential element in education that lights a fire in learners. It is equally essential in schooling that is based on the Three D's of Success.

Invitational help is the unifying force that ties the success model to the framework for lighting the fire. When the teacher invites students to achieve the ultimate goal of the course, explaining how the student just can't live without achieving this goal, the teacher is helping the student with learning outcomes. When a teacher asks a student to think about setting a personal goal that will lead to success with the ultimate learning outcome, the teacher is helping the student with desire. When the teacher further invites a student to decide to achieve that goal, the teacher is helping the student make a decision. These are not the typical activities that come to mind when teachers think about providing help to their students.

Help That Instructs

More familiar to teachers than help that invites is help that instructs.

Instructional help forms the nexus between the "learning activities" element of the lighting the fire framework and the "determination" part of the Three D's of Success model. Once students have set a goal and decided to achieve it, they need help in developing the skills to sustain them through the determination phase of learning. Usually this means providing help to students so that they can become proficient at *doing* what they need to do to achieve their goal (see Inouye, Merrill, & Swan, 2004). Teachers typically have a storehouse of methods and techniques for helping students develop the needed skills. The key that we are emphasizing here is that this kind of instructional help needs to be constantly aimed at both lighting a fire in the learner and helping the learner achieve success.

I assure my students when I teach a new concept that I don't expect full understanding the first time I present a learning activity. Gardner (2006) in his work on multiple intelligences theorizes that we all have different learning styles. I suppose it would be nice to include all seven learning styles in every lesson, but my goal is to try to teach a concept seven times in seven different ways (personal communication, Quentin L. Cook, September 15, 2007). I rehearse to my students:

This is just the first time, now let's try it another way and then tomorrow we'll review using a different method. Don't panic if you don't understand the first time. When we've done something seven times in seven different ways, then we'll have real understanding.

HELP THAT CONFIRMS

In addition to help that invites and help that instructs, a third type of help is essential to lighting a fire and helping students succeed: help that confirms. Teachers often provide this type of help but may not do it consciously. We are not talking here about simple praise or encouragement, although those forms of confirming help can be effective. We are referring to the kind of help a teacher gives when she convinces the student that success has been reached. Confirmatory help ties learning assessments from lighting a fire together with success and expectations from the Three D's. When a teacher uses data from an assignment or test to convince a student that success is not only possible but inevitable, the teacher is providing help that confirms. Then when the success comes, so does a celebration of the success—again confirming the results to the learner. Finally, the teacher can help the learners look to the future and raise their expectations for what is possible following each success.

Billy, as we will call him, a sixth-grade student who said he wanted to be a thoracic surgeon, needed all three kinds of help—help that *invites, instructs,* and *confirms.* One glance at Billy's spelling booklet and I wondered if he might have a writing disability. I had to use all the imagination I could muster to see a resemblance between his scratches on the paper and the words for the weekly spelling test. After Billy failed two tests and I had repeatedly requested that he redo the tests, I called his mother and enlisted her help. She seemed reluctant but was appreciative of the call and said she would work with him. That same week I had also asked my students to have a responsible adult read their vocabulary sentences and proof them for capitals, punctuation, and meaningfulness.

For four consecutive days, Billy couldn't remember to ask his mother to check his words with him. Instead of expressing disappointment in his choice to forget, I decided to help him one morning during silent reading time. We went over every word. I encouraged him as he found mistakes and laughed when he couldn't read his own writing. We talked about the purpose of the assignment—that it was not to fill the spaces with nearly undecipherable pencil markings but to write real words that communicated meaning. I explained that I wanted him to be able to write his thoughts and ideas so that he could fulfill his dream of becoming a thoracic surgeon.

As I saw him succeed in writing legibly and spelling his words correctly, I praised him and then told him, "Now that I know you can write, you can never fool me again. I will help you learn the spelling rules you missed when you were younger." Later that same day, I corrected his spelling test, and he got 100 percent. Billy asked if he could keep his spelling test book to show his mother when she came to our class for an activity. She told me privately that she had given up on him, but when she saw his latest test, she knew, as did I, that he could succeed.

Although I was not consciously thinking of the three kinds of help as I tried to assist Billy, all three occurred. I invited him to set a goal to spell better so that he could one day reach his goal of becoming a thoracic surgeon; I was trying to strengthen his *desire* to learn by linking the goal with his life. Then I invited him to do his very best rather than just writing anything at all on the paper. I was really asking him to make a firm *decision* to achieve the goal he wanted to achieve. When I was working with him alone on his spelling, I was using a *learning activity* to build his skill so that his *determination* would actually lead to better results on the spelling test—the nature of instructional help. Finally, when I celebrated with him when he got a 100 percent on the test, I was *confirming* his *success,* and I talked to him about what he anticipated in the future and confirmed to him that his expectations were higher than they were before he had succeeded. Billy's example shows how the Three D's model and lighting the fire framework tie together.

Another example using older students helps illustrate the power of giving the right kind of help to students. John Bell, a biology professor at a major university, decided that he wanted to try teaching the introductory biology course differently from the way it is taught at most universities. The typical approach generally includes assigning readings in the textbook, lecturing on the topic of the assigned readings, asking students to complete the end-of-chapter exercises, and then sending them to the university's testing center to complete the midterm and final exams—the filling-a-bucket approach. Discussions with colleagues around the country convinced him that many students felt a strong disdain for science and enrolled only because they had to get the credit to graduate.

During the previous semester when students were registering for their courses, he advertised his section as being designed for "those who hate science." Eighty-one students enrolled in the course. On the first day he asked how many had actually seen the ad and registered for the course because they hated science. Three-fourths of the students raised their hands. He then asked them why they hated science. In his words, "We talked for most of the class period about their reasons, and all of the reasons focused on pedagogy. They didn't hate the content, they just hated the way it had been taught to them before they arrived at the university." John then told the students that he would not be satisfied if they simply felt less negative about biology at the end of the semester. He did not want them just to tolerate it; he wanted them to love it.

He then explained that there would be no traditional tests, no long lists of words to memorize, no chapter reviews. Instead, he explained, "I want you to come up with your own questions about biology—questions that relate to your life, questions you would like to find answers to." The students then submitted their questions. John combined similar questions so that there were a total of nine student-requested topics. Following several weeks of preparatory study of basic concepts in biology, students produced a brief research paper every week on one of the nine topics until they had answered all of them. On Fridays students brought their rough draft of the paper they had produced after doing their library research and critiqued each other's papers, with teaching assistants and the teacher providing instructional help.

Every Monday they handed in their final papers that were graded for their adherence to scientific principles of research and the clarity of the explanations of biological concepts. At the end of the course John congratulated his students for their performance by asking them if they would be willing to take a biology final exam in an essay format: "I know I told you that I would not give any traditional tests in the course," he explained, "but I think you've learned so much biology that I would like to see how you would do. Would you be willing to take the exam?" The students all agreed. Their performance on the exam, just as John had hoped, was excellent, even though they had not done anything additional to prepare for the experience other than writing the brief research papers.

We like this example because help was always on the way in this class. The teacher began by helping students face their negative perceptions about the content of the course. He was clearly inviting them to reconsider their own attitudes. He was trying to light a fire. He was also trying to help them increase their *desire*. When he asked them to come up with their own questions, he was causing them to make *decisions* about their learning. When he told them that he wanted to turn their hate of science into love, he was raising their sights to a much higher level of *learning outcomes* than most students had ever encountered.

He knew that their knowledge of biology was not deep, so he provided instruction early in the semester to give them a good foundation—just enough to provide them with the tools they needed to succeed in their individual research. Later, when they were writing their papers, he provided help from peers, teaching assistants, and the instructor to ensure that students' determination would lead to success. His *learning activities* were very different from the traditional assignments and exams because he was trying to light a fire and not just fill a bucket.

At the end of the semester, when all the student papers had been turned in, he recognized the quality of students' research and confirmed to them how much he felt they had learned. He was so excited about their performance that he gave even more confirmatory help by asking if they wanted to take a final exam. If he had told students about that final exam at the beginning of the semester, he knew that most would not have looked forward with great anticipation to taking it, but he also knew that some of his colleagues might wonder about a course that did not have a traditional final. So he let his students make the decision. He expressed his confidence in them—a form of help that confirms—and then asked them to take the test. So they chose to take a test that they had not planned on completing. Their expectations of success were high because they recognized, as did the instructor, that they had learned a great deal, so they wanted to demonstrate their newfound knowledge.

THINK IT, CHOOSE IT, DO IT, SUCCEED

When teachers use the Three D's and the lighting the fire framework as tools to improve their teaching, we are confident that learning will increase. The primary role of a teacher is to provide help. If, however, a teacher sees instructional help as the only kind of help, students will make far less progress, experience far less success, and may not feel the excitement of a fire being lit. We like to shorten the Three D's model to "Think it, Choose it, Do it, Succeed." These should be the guiding forces that teachers consider as they try to help students reach their goals. To succeed means that students need to feel stronger, more able, more skilled, and more knowledgeable. Students will not choose to learn unless they feel that success is possible. They will give up, much as Billy had given up on his writing or as the biology students had given up on science.

Each of the three types of help we have discussed in this chapter focuses on strengthening the student. Effective invitations strengthen. They convince the learners that they can do more than they thought possible. Effective instruction strengthens because it develops or polishes skills needed to succeed, and confirmatory help strengthens. It communicates confidence to the learner. When I asked a group of faculty to identify past teachers who had helped light their fire for learning, the most common characteristic mentioned was "the teacher expressed confidence in me." An effective teacher confirms to students that they can accomplish more than they ever thought possible.

Help that fills the bucket is nothing more than information dissemination. The teacher spews out concept after concept, and the student tries to listen, understand, and then give the knowledge back on a test. The metaphor of the bucket is particularly troubling because the purpose of tests in such a system is to ask the student to empty the bucket after it is full, and once it is empty, the knowledge is gone.

I once asked students to tell me about their most positive, fulfilling learning experiences and then contrast those experiences with their most negative, frustrating ones. One student, describing her most frustrating experience, recounted how she had gone to a teacher for help, and the teacher rudely refused to give it to her. She said, "I never wanted to go to class again." And then she ended her account with a rather surprising afterthought: "You know, I can't even remember what the topic of the class was. I have repressed the experience so much. I don't even know what I was supposed to be learning" (see Top & Osguthorpe, 1985).

Given that she had taken the class only a year or two before she responded to my questionnaire, it was obvious that her bucket was totally empty. She was, at least in this class, addicted to failure. The fundamental necessity of a good student-teacher relationship had been breeched, and she had been permanently turned off—so turned off she couldn't even remember what she was turned off to. Not exactly lighting a fire. She went for help, and help was not to be found. Now, we realize that the teacher might have had another view of the situation. Perhaps this student was not the most responsible member of the class. We don't know, but we do know that formal schooling is often full of these kinds of experiences and that students and teachers alike suffer because of it.

The solution, we believe, is not complex. It can be summarized in three words: choose to learn. The student's responsibility is to exercise personal agency and decide to reach a worthy learning goal. The teacher's responsibility is actually twofold: (1) choose to keep learning themselves—to keep their own fire burning, and (2) choose to provide the kind of help that will lead students to success.

MAKING IT HAPPEN

- **Invite reluctant learners.** Reluctant learners are those who are addicted to failure or are on their way to becoming addicted. They're satisfied with performance that is less than their best. It is easy to invite students who are eager to learn, but when a learner is reluctant, we suggest that you become more strategic in giving help that invites. Seat the reluctant learner next to a student who will help rather than distract. Prove to reluctant learners that they are more capable than they think—not by simple praise but by showing them hard evidence that they can achieve the learning goal. Consider peer, cross-age, and adult tutors or parents to add to your arsenal of help. Give these tutors specific learning activities to complete with reluctant learners. They need to be trained to guide the learner to mastery and not accept less than the learner's best efforts. The tutor's or teacher's job is to help reluctant learners feel good about doing their very best— not to help them feel satisfied with less than that. Tutors need specific training so that they do not overprompt or do the task for the learner. This training needs to be accomplished by the teacher through role-playing and demonstrating how to give appropriate instructional help to reluctant learners.

• **"I will help only if you need it."** Instructional help is often neither instructional nor helpful. Examine each learning activity. Ask yourself the following questions:

1. Is the learning activity linked to the desired outcome and the assessment?

2. Is the learning activity in the "zone of attainable success"? Is it both challenging and attainable?

3. Does the learning activity wean the learner from instructional help? Is overprompting avoided?

4. Do students who succeed on the learning activity succeed on the final measure of the learning outcome?

When you are reading with a student, you might say, "I will help you only if you need it." Your goal is to build independence in the student. However, if a student continually makes mistakes in reading without receiving effective help, that student will need to unlearn those mistakes, which is far more difficult than providing the right help in the first place.

• **Encourage peer help.** Help students understand that they have a responsibility for their own learning. They need to do assignments, turn them in on time, prepare for tests, and so on. However, they also have a responsibility to help others. If they finish an in-class assignment early, they should look around to see if anyone else needs help. Encourage collaboration and discourage competition between students. Help students understand that competition is helpful in learning when you are competing with yourself. You always want to try harder, do better than you did previously, but comparing your own performance with that of others is pointless and sometimes destructive. Teach students that they all have the capacity to help other students and that if they really want to become expert at anything they will achieve that expertise much faster if they help someone else learn it along the way.

- **Confirm success individually and to the class.**
Develop a culture of confirmation in your classroom. To do this, you must systematically search for examples of student success. When the whole class gets a higher mean score on any test, you confirm that success by showing the class how the current performance compares with the past. This whole-class confirmation method could be done as follows:

> I just graded the test, and guess what? We have set a new record. This is the first time we scored an average of over 90 percent on this test and no one scored below 80 percent. I knew you could do it, and you did. At the beginning of the year, the average was 70 percent, and there were students who didn't get even half the answers correct. Do you think I'm more excited about this 90 percent average or that everyone scored above 80 percent?

Communicate to students that when one or two students do well, that is a good thing for those students, but when the whole class makes progress, that is the ultimate success. When you provide confirmatory help to the whole group, you subtly communicate that you have confidence in everyone. You write off no one. Everyone feels validated. Everyone feels needed.

6

Do the Right Thing for the Right Reason

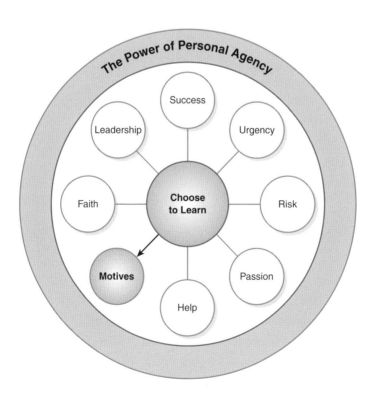

The Power of Personal Agency

Success

Leadership

Urgency

Faith

Choose to Learn

Risk

Motives

Passion

Help

Everyone approaches learning and teaching a little bit differently. Consider the following imaginary cases:

Kimberly: A pleasant, friendly ninth grader, Kimberly is socially skilled but likes to hang out with her friends more than she likes to do her homework. Whenever her friends call, she goes with them. Her grades at school are not all that bad, but she is functioning well below her potential as a student. If asked about her less-than-stellar performance at school, she just smiles and responds, "Like I don't really care that much about school."

Robert: Most think of Robert as a fifth grader with ADHD. He has a hard time attending in class and is socially awkward. He thinks about only one thing: playing video games. As soon as he gets home, he hits the computer and stays on it until his parents come home from work three hours later.

Maggie: A principal of a junior high school, Maggie has become in her words, "just plain tired of it all." She's had police officers in her building three times during the past two weeks gathering evidence for a crime two of her students allegedly committed. She has a former teacher who is trying to sue the school for sexual harassment, and she just found out that the school will lose funding because she did not submit a report to the district on time.

Although Kimberly, Robert, and Maggie are different in many ways, they all have one thing in common: they have quit trying. Kimberly has quit trying to do well in school. Robert has quit trying to pay attention, and Maggie has quit trying to lead as the principal in her school. They are all yielding to an addiction to failure. Even though their yielding has not been totally conscious at times, they have gradually chosen to be addicted.

The original meaning of the word *addiction* in Roman law was "a surrender or dedication of anyone to a master." Kimberly surrendered to her friends and their social agenda. Robert surrendered to video games. And Maggie? What did Maggie surrender to? We will say that Maggie surrendered to life's negative pressures. She was overcome with problems and let them conquer her.

A teacher can be overcome with addictions. A student can be overcome, and so can a principal. Addictions to failure come in every form. Some are obvious—a teacher who becomes addicted to prescription pain medications fails to show up for work. But most addictions to failure are more subtle. Most don't even consider them addictions at all. However, when people yield to anything that keeps them from learning, they are becoming addicted to failure. Anytime students become content to achieve much less than they are capable of achieving, they are addicted to failure.

I direct a center at my university with the goal of improving student learning on the entire campus. That means helping faculty to improve their teaching. One way to assess the quality of teaching is to ask students how much they learned in a course. If most students in a course say they learned very little because the course was poorly taught, that faculty member usually needs some help. Some faculty who get negative reviews on their teaching are eager to improve and seek the center's help. A few avoid getting the help they need. A department chair might say, "I've tried to get that faculty member to come to your center, but he won't. He says it's too humiliating to submit himself to that kind of evaluation."

In the previous chapter we explained that good teachers always need to communicate to learners that help is on the way. But if learners won't access the help, then what? No one can force another person to learn. Learning is an act of choice. So anytime students or teachers—even senior university faculty—refuse help that they so obviously need, they are addicted to failure. They have stopped trying to improve. They have chosen *not* to learn. And what about the department chair or school principal who does nothing? That person has yielded as well to the addiction to failure. When a leader gives up on a person the leader is supposed to be helping, the leader has written off that person.

What does it mean to write somebody off? It means to ignore the person and the problems that the person needs to solve. It equals neglect. A parent can be overcome with the problems of a child, but if the parent gives up, the parent has yielded to the addiction to failure. The parent has chosen to support the child's problems—even foster the problems—by doing nothing. When teachers say to themselves—even subconsciously—that they don't believe they can help a student, the teachers have yielded to failure, a double failure—failure for the teacher and failure for the student who is written off.

The Opposite of an Addiction to Failure

Some might conclude that the opposite of an addiction to failure is an addiction to success or an addiction to learning. In the strict definition of the word *addiction* this is correct (see Schaler, 2000). You can be devoted to good things as well as to bad things. We believe, however, that this definition does not focus forcefully enough on the role of personal agency in addiction. For us, *addiction* means to give up one's agency, to stop making rational choices and allow an external attraction to rule one's will. The teacher who is doing poorly and refuses help has made an irrational choice that leads to negative results for both student and teacher. It would be like a patient diagnosed with a staph infection refusing to take an antibiotic. Addiction is centered on the act of "surrender." And what do addicts surrender? Their will, their power to choose the good.

On a recent visit to a hospital we saw a man exiting with his oxygen tank trailing behind him. He obviously had some type of lung disease. After sitting down on a bench by the entrance to the hospital, he lit his cigarette and began to smoke with the oxygen tubes still in his nose. We're sure that if we had asked him, he would have said that he wished he had never begun smoking. He was still unable to quit. No doubt doctors had told him that if he did not stop smoking, he would shorten his life significantly, but his will apparently had been surrendered to the substance between his fingers. A four-inch roll of weed was ruling him.

So what is the opposite of an addiction to failure? It is *choosing to learn.* It is taking control of the most important human quality with which anyone is endowed: personal agency, the power to choose. Learning itself is an act of agency. Learning is a personal choice. In our minds learning is much more than "acquiring knowledge," the traditional meaning of the word. It is giving up a former way of thinking and trading it in for a new and better way (Osguthorpe, 1996). In the success-oriented approach to learning, the learner finally rejects the notion that the learning goal was impossible.

In one sense, then, learning is an act of discarding bad behavior and replacing it with the good. When the Nobel Prize winners in medicine proved that a gene could be disabled or "turned off," the funding agency who had originally denied Capecchi and others support had to correct their previous conclusion that it was impossible. Everyone eventually accepted the finding, but in the beginning it was really the prize winners themselves who chose to learn.

That is why the opposite of an addiction to failure is to choose to learn. Every time a student or a teacher refuses to yield to failure—to write someone or some problem off—that student or teacher is choosing to learn. They are saying, in essence, "We know that some think what we are trying to do is not possible. We have thought it at times, but we simply won't give up. We will keep trying."

The act of trying is an act of choosing to learn. The one who stops trying has yielded to failure. The one who keeps trying refuses to yield and keeps choosing to learn. These are two simple choices: one leads to greater personal strength, the other to weakness. One promotes health in oneself and others, while the other causes frustration and despair. The choices do more than determine the grade one will receive in a course.

The choice to learn or to be addicted to failure determines the kind of person one will become, the kind of life one will lead.

MOTIVES AND ACTIONS

Table 6.1 shows that motives are at least as important in learning as are the actions one takes to learn or the results of such actions. Choosing to learn means doing the right thing for the right reason.

Learners in the "choose to learn" box have pure motives—they want to learn, their desire is aimed at a worthy goal. They are applying themselves effectively to the task at hand. They are choosing to learn (see Osguthorpe, in press). Those in the "choose to forget" box have the same desire, the same motives, even possibly the same goals as those in the "choose to learn" box, but they periodically forget who they are and what they can accomplish. They momentarily settle for less than their best. They might lose patience with themselves or with others. They might get distracted at times, but because their motives are pure, they wake up and remember that they can still choose to learn. Most of us go back and forth between these two boxes. We all make mistakes from time to time. We all forget that we were really meant to succeed in life.

Table 6.1   Do the Right Thing for the Right Reason

		Motives	
		Pure	Impure
A c t i o n s	*Successful*	*Choose to learn*	Choose to deceive
	Unsuccessful	Choose to forget	Choose to fail

Those in the "choose to deceive" box are in more trouble. They pass their tests, but they may cheat in the process. These students have impure motives and often deceive themselves as well as the teacher. Their motive might be to make others in the class look less competent then they are, or they might be interested only in getting a good grade. Whether they cheat or whether they try to put others down, they are not choosing to learn.

Those in the "choose to fail" box have chosen an addiction to failure. They know they are doing poorly, and they don't care. They've given up. They don't even try to deceive anyone. Sometimes they even look proud of their choice to do poorly. Failure becomes their identity. If they began to do well, they—at least in their own minds—would lose their friends and become insecure in a world of do-gooders. So they consciously choose to keep failing. They may not be deceiving those around them, but they are deceiving themselves (see Arbinger Institute, 2002).

Taken to the extreme, the ones who continue on the path of choosing to deceive might become successful business leaders who eventually defraud their coworkers. Those in the "choose to fail" box who are openly proud of their failure might one day populate our prisons. This is why the stakes are so high in education. The child who is really "left behind" in the system is not the one who gets a few low scores on a test. Rather it is the child who never knows what it means to achieve a worthy goal once thought impossible.

The Three D's of Success

The Three D's of Success is a tool for teachers to help students choose to learn. Those who slip into the "choose to forget" box may still be trying. They have the desire to learn. They've even made a decision to learn, but their determination flags at times. Primarily they need instructional help. Those in the "choose to deceive" box are suffering from goal confusion. They've become mixed up about the purpose of education.

Their desires are warped. They don't really need instructional help. They are already succeeding on school tasks. They need help that invites, and the invitation needs to carry with it persuasion so that they can see how they are deceiving themselves as well as others. The only way for a teacher to help such a student is to recognize the deception and to help the student recognize it. Even the smallest bit of progress then needs to be confirmed by the teacher.

Those in the "choose to fail" box need all kinds of help. Their desires are mixed up. They have decided to avoid learning and to avoid achieving any worthy goal, and their determination is aimed at failure. They're addicted and don't know it. Instructional help is quite useless for them. Confirmatory help is also not possible, because they have no achievement worthy of confirmation. Invitational help is the focus here. They need to be invited to give up their addiction to failure. Not an easy task, but much more critical than the usual types of instructional help on which teachers focus.

LIGHTING THE FIRE

The light the fire framework, like the Three D's of Success, is a lens for teachers to examine their practice. There is an underlying assumption in the framework that students are not already addicted to failure. Invitational help needs to precede much of the effort that goes into lighting a fire in students. The most important element in the framework, when thinking about students' motives, is the foundation of edifying relationships.

One of the definitions of *invite* is that the one giving the invitation *assumes* that the one who receives it will accept the invitation. One typically does not invite a stranger to one's birthday party. The invitations go out to close friends and family members. Likewise the invitations that teachers give to students are effective only to the degree to which a positive edifying relationship has been formed. The teacher knows how to invite the hard-to-reach student, because the teacher understands the student, and the student understands the teacher. And the student knows that the teacher knows.

Only at this point can a teacher give an invitation to a student to learn and *assume* that the student will accept it. The invitation will be the right one because the relationship has already been established. For students with impure motives, the process of inviting is complicated but so essential to the students' success. Each invitation accepted means that the flame for learning in the student is burning brighter.

CAN ONE JUDGE ANOTHER'S MOTIVES?

Doing the right thing for the right reason means examining our own motives. During a presentation at a national meeting of educational researchers, a participant raised his hand and, with an edge in his voice, challenged me with the following question:

> So how can you judge another's motives? It seems as if you are suggesting that teachers not only assess what their students are doing, but they're also supposed to be able to tell why they're doing it. Isn't that a job for God?

I assured the questioner that I was not suggesting that teachers or educational testing firms develop instruments to measure students' motives. Then I said, "You're right, it is a dangerous thing to attribute motives to another person, but we can understand our own motives, and we can judge them ourselves."

It is this type of inviting that students who are addicted to failure need so desperately. They need an invitation from a trusted adult to examine their own motives, their own lives, and to decide to change. No one can make the changes for them. They must exercise their own agency, but without an invitation—the right invitation—many will continue in their addiction.

All three of our imaginary cases at the beginning of this chapter could certainly, if given the proper invitation, examine their own motives. In the process they would likely discover that their motives were less than the highest in them.

Kimberly would recognize that performing well below her potential would not lead to the kind of life she wanted. Robert would see that video games were taking over his life. Maggie would come to understand that giving up on her school was not a desirable option for her or for those she had been assigned to lead. All three had some motive problems that they needed to figure out for themselves. However, others close to them—those with nurturing relationships—could help invite them to change, to begin doing the right thing for the right reason. They could help them choose to learn.

MAKING IT HAPPEN

• **Encourage students to examine their own motives.** A favorite teacher of ours who taught at an alternative high school in California asked her students to give themselves four different grades on each assignment after they had received their mastery score. The four grades were for "attitude," "concentration," "self-control," and "honesty." The teacher was trying to help her students do the right thing for the right reason. You could ask your students to do the same. After they receive a score or grade from you on any assignment, try asking them to rate themselves on attitude, concentration, self-control, and honesty. If they did the assignment with excitement, they could give themselves an A for attitude. If they really focused—exerted a lot of effort—they could give themselves an A for concentration, and so on. Of particular interest is the category of "honesty." This was the grade the teacher found most powerful for students. This caused her students to self-evaluate and determine *why* they did the assignment, not just how well they performed. Did they cheat or consider cheating? Did they do it half-heartedly? Did they do their very best? If not, they were not honest. She praised them when they were honest, even if they did not do well on the assignment. She put a chart on her wall with the four words on it and referred to it often—a good strategy to help students do the right thing for the right reason.

• **Teach honestly.** Teachers can benefit, just as students can, from evaluating their own motives. We are convinced that teachers who suffer from burnout are not in the "choose to learn" box in Table 6.1. They may suffer from self-deception and, at times, from deceiving others. Their heart may not be in the work, and so they gradually detach themselves from it altogether. Because the classroom is a place where teachers and students are constantly making decisions, it is a place to learn the virtues. We suggest that moral education is most effectively accomplished by applying the virtues themselves in the practice of learning and teaching. So rather than giving a lesson on honesty, teach in honest ways and expect students to learn in honest ways. Rather than giving a lesson on caring, teach and learn in caring ways. So examine your own motives, your own teaching methods, and your own expectations for students as they learn. Bring your own motives and actions into congruence, and help your students do the same. You might choose to use Table 6.1 to help students examine their own motives and actions. You might place it on the wall and refer to it, especially when you notice students choosing to learn.

• **Learn from your mistakes.** After watching one of our children lose a close basketball game, we approached her and said, "Well, it was close, and you played well, but your team can always learn something from a loss." She quickly responded,

> I don't think so. You don't learn anything if you don't do your very best, and some members of our team were not doing their best because they really did not expect to win. They just made excuses because they thought the other team was better. But we really could have beat the team if we had just believed we could.

Show Table 6.1 to your students and point to the "choose to forget" box, then say,

> You know, when you choose to forget, you are really not trying to remember. The only way for you to come back into the "choose to learn" box is to do your best.

It's perfectly all right to make mistakes when you're trying, but when you say, "I forgot to do that assignment," you're not really trying to do your best, are you? You're choosing to forget. You're excusing yourself. It's so easy to get back into the "choose to learn" box. All you have to do is stop forgetting and choose to remember. Begin trying to do your best.

• **Do your very best, and your best gets better.** A well-known injunction is "Do your very best." Help your students understand that when they do their very best—when they really try—then their best gets better. That's what the "choose to learn" box in Table 6.1 is all about. Learning is succeeding at something, and the only way to succeed is to give it your all. Otherwise you don't know how well you might have done. In our experience most students, most people for that matter, seldom do their very best. When students seem to go beyond themselves, when they actually seem surprised at their own performance, you can confirm it by showing evidence and helping them see that they actually did their very best. Then use the Three D's to show them how their best will get better, because once a student has accomplished a difficult task, it is no longer difficult. The student will want to attempt something more challenging the next time, and the student's best will get better.

7

Extinguish
the Negative

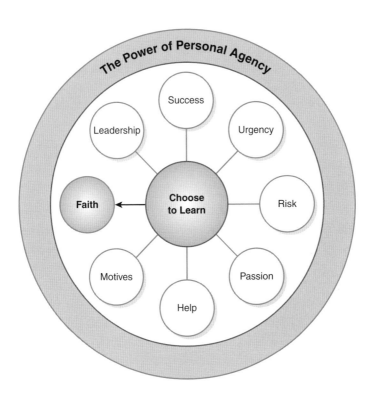

Hanging on our wall is a picture of a café located at the intersection of two state roads near Edgerton, Wyoming. It is a small, square, flat-roofed structure with red shake shingles above two cluttered bay windows. It looks like a piece of scenery from an old Western movie, except for the oil derrick and pick-up trucks in the parking lot. Its name: "Whiners Café." The story told to us is that those working in the oil fields that surround the café would come there every day to complain about their jobs. So the owner decided to acknowledge the café's function in the community—a place to come and whine.

Whining is not unique to oil field workers in Wyoming. It afflicts nearly everyone. Teachers, students, and principals are all susceptible to it. If teachers get together for lunch and start complaining, a principal might be tempted to put a sign up over the lunchroom: "Whiners Café." But principals often have the same problem when they get together, so the sign would need to be portable!

When we conduct seminars on teaching and learning, I put on a gas mask and pick up my extinguisher. I then approach a conference participant and ask, "So have you heard anything negative recently?" The participant always comes up with something quickly, such as, "We never have time to do what we need to do," or "We have to give too many tests. If we didn't have to test so much, maybe we would have time to teach!" Then I spray the extinguisher and exclaim, "Extinguish that negative talk."

Whining never leads anywhere productive—just to a place like Whiners Café where people try to one-up each other with negative talk. Students fall prey to it at every level of schooling. They can be heard to talk negatively of classmates, of teachers, of assignments, of grades, and, most importantly, of themselves. Such talk can eventually lead to an addiction to failure. Students can talk themselves into the belief that failure is their only option.

Make No Excuses

A special and subtle type of negative talk occurs when people make excuses. The reason that excuse making is often so subtle is that people believe that all they are doing is stating a fact, such as, "We can't build the new addition to the building because the leeway didn't pass, so we're still going to have too many in our classes." This doesn't sound like an excuse. It sounds like a statement of a fact. The leeway did not pass. The addition to the building will not be built. Class size will remain large. Lurking beneath such a simple statement, however, is the unstated feeling that I will not be able to teach as well as I need to be able to teach because of these uncontrollable external constraints.

A student might engage in the same type of excuse making. For example, a student might say, "I had soccer practice after school, and then I went to a birthday party for my cousin, and so I didn't have time to do my homework last night." The student actually did have soccer practice and actually did go to a birthday party. Again, however, the student did not see this as making an excuse.

The teacher and student in these examples both fail to see that their excuse making is limiting their own power to choose. Each excuse a person makes causes success to be a little farther out of reach. We recognize the existence of external constraints that cause educators and students difficulty. But no fire can be lit in a teacher or a student who keeps making excuses. Excuses diminish the excuse maker and often the one listening to the excuses. Imagine how long the day must have been for the owner of the Whiners Café—listening all day to people come in and whine about their lot in life. Those who choose to learn choose not to whine. Rather, they find ways to solve the seemingly unsolvable. They work their way to success in spite of any obstacle that confronts them. The alternative, then, to excuse making and negative talk of any kind is to develop faith that success will come.

AN EYE OF FAITH

Dusting my neglected bookshelves at home one Saturday afternoon, I stumbled across a children's book titled *The Spyglass* by Richard Paul Evans (2000). While we had been away from our home for an extended period, our daughter had received the book as a gift from a friend and had left it in our library. Always looking for a good read-aloud for my sixth graders, I stopped to read the book. The illustrations by Jonathan Linton were elegant and immediately drew me into this new parable about seeing the world through an eye of faith.

The king in this story rules over a poor kingdom with subjects who are also poor in spirit. An old man seeking shelter bluntly tells the king that he doesn't look like a great ruler and that he should change. With the help of a spyglass, the old man shows the king what his kingdom could become. The king embarks on a journey through the kingdom to show his subjects what it means to see with an eye of faith and shows them what they might become. When the old man returns for the spyglass, the king doesn't want to give it up, but the old man tells the king he no longer needs it. The old man says, "The spyglass only showed you what could be if you believed, for it was only faith that you and your people lacked." He goes on to explain, "Only with faith can we see that which is not, but can be. The eye of faith is greater than the natural eye, for the natural eye sees only a portion of truth. The eye of faith sees without bounds or limits."

Parables such as *The Spyglass* are understood on many levels, but my sixth graders understand this invitation to see with an eye of faith. We talk often about setting goals that are beyond anything they have thus far accomplished. Weekly they set a goal that is reachable and attainable but also stretches them beyond what they have done before. Everyone's goal is different, but we also have class goals such as every student earns 100 percent on the weekly spelling test or every student in the class returns their reading log with a parent signature.

These class goals are reachable and attainable, but they also stretch each class member. No excuses are accepted. No negative talk. I tell my class that my goal is to have *every* student succeed, not just the ones who have an easy time with schoolwork.

HELP AND FAITH

Assisting students to see with an eye of faith demands all three kinds of help: inviting, instructing, and confirming. One day I greeted a student passing by my office. He said, "I don't have that assignment done yet because I'm just not good at this kind of thing." I asked him to sit down in my office. "I hope you will never say that again," I implored. "Never say you can't do it. If you are having trouble, let's find out what the trouble is and move on, but don't ever voice a lack of faith in yourself." He was a little surprised at my counsel, but I was trying to invite him to eliminate negative talk about himself—a type of excuse— so that he could make progress toward his goal.

I was not focusing on this student's self-esteem. I did not praise him for doing nothing. I invited him to make a decision to succeed. We talked for several minutes about the multiple frustrations he was having in his education. We found some things that he could accomplish right then, that day. He went out, accomplished them, and felt much better. His negative self-talk was dragging him down. He needed someone to pick him back up. I do not believe that it would have helped him to agree with him, empathize with his plight, or excuse him from the assignment. He needed strengthening help. He needed to regain the faith that he could progress toward his goal. So I tried to provide the invitation, the instructional help, and the confirmatory help when he had finally achieved his goal.

What happens when, instead of receiving help that confirms, a student continually receives feedback that shows the student is not succeeding? What if the results of learning attempts show that the student is gradually getting worse instead of better? This is not help that confirms. It is really not help at all. Rather, it can be discouraging for the student unless a teacher intervenes and interprets it. In the absence of a teacher's explanation, some students will likely conclude that they are simply not meant to succeed in this particular area. If a high jumper found that the more he practiced, the worse he became, he would likely stop practicing. He would also likely invent reasons for his failures. Negative evidence usually causes people to enter an endless and often fruitless cycle of explaining away the poor performance. Doing worse shows the learner that the vision once sought is now out of reach.

Help, then, needs to confirm successes however small they might be in the beginning. Any improvement is worth heralding, any progress worth confirming. If the success does not seem to come, the teacher needs to change the instructional help so that success can be achieved. Regardless of how small the success, the teacher's role is to help students achieve it. Periodic setbacks need to be viewed as temporary. There is no need to develop a complex set of explanations for the poor performance. Rather, consider the poor performance as a stepping stone on the way to success, a bump in the path. Then the next practice session will be better, and the vision will stay in view and remain reachable.

We are not suggesting that teachers look at their students' performance through rose-colored glasses, that they ignore poor performance, or that they pretend everything is all right when it is not. Rather, we believe, as does Collins (2005), that you must "confront the most brutal facts of your current reality, but maintain unwavering faith that you can prevail in the end" (p. 13). He developed this principle after examining the eleven highest performing corporations in the Fortune 500. But the principle applies equally well to the classroom. If a teacher wants "greatness" from students, just as a business leader wants "greatness" from employees, the teacher must recognize poor performance (the "brutal facts") and then help the student gain the confidence needed to succeed ("unwavering faith").

VISION AND FAITH

The *Spyglass* story emphasizes the importance of vision and its relationship to faith. You have to see it before you can accomplish it. Oftentimes students' main problem is that they cannot *imagine* themselves achieving the goal (see Greene, 2000). One reason they cannot imagine it is because a goal might keep changing the closer they approach it.

As students' performance in my math class gradually increased, the more I noticed that their goal kept rising. We decided as a group that anyone scoring below 80 percent on the end-of-chapter test would need to retake it and demonstrate understanding. We wanted everyone in the class to understand the concepts we were learning. Gradually this goal increased to 90 percent in the minds of the students because they realized that they needed to understand every little nuance and leave room for only a "silly little mistake." I kept telling them I was interested in only one thing: helping them learn and love math. So I invited them to retake a form of the test as many times as they would like to show themselves they understood the concepts. Scores increased, and 100 percent became the mode or most common score earned in our class even without retakes.

One low-achieving student thinking of transferring to a regular sixth-grade math class resubmitted assignments for mastery, stayed after school for help, and asked her mother to tutor her and help her prepare for tests (something she had previously resisted). For the first time in her life, she said that she understood math and that it made sense to her. When she earned a 95 percent on the last chapter test, she couldn't wipe the smile off her face.

Vision can be individual, group, or organizational. An individual can have a vision of becoming successful in algebra, or the whole group of students might have that vision. A group of teachers might have a vision that they can help every student improve their reading proficiency by more than one grade level. A school might have a vision that all students will pass the state core exams. If any of these goals has been achieved previously, the goals do not really constitute a vision. A vision is something yet unrealized. If the goals have been previously achieved, no faith is needed. Everyone already knows that it is possible.

A vision must cause people to reach beyond their present circumstance. That is why we define success as achieving something that you previously thought was impossible—doing better than you think you can do. This definition of success requires a vision, and it requires faith. A fire cannot be lit in a learner if the learner has already achieved the goal. Reaching for the seemingly unattainable—this is what learning is all about.

Consider the following unedited examples from my class of students' journal entries:

- **Student 1.** A sixth-grade student who speaks English as a second language:

  I'm getting better at math, sometimes i don't no what to do but this is normal, i'm getting better at writing to, but some times i don't no how to spell but some day i well know how to spell every think, i believe i can do it.

  My dream is one day be a artist, and i want to draw perfect and i want to play violin realy good. i'm goin to work on this thinks and get better. i know i can do it if i work on it.

- **Student 2.** A sixth-grade student who speaks two languages fluently:

  I think this is the best project I've ever done! I think I'm going to have a 4 on this one because I put so much work in it. It's probably really the first time I've ever really done that before! I think I'm going to do great because Mrs. Osguthorpe is always telling us that we have to try our very best in everything and because of that I've been doing better this year than any other year. I think this is going to be my best year.

Both of these students realize that they have much to learn, but both are beginning to see that success is possible. They don't make excuses. They have extinguished the negative. They are developing the vision and faith to reach it.

MAKING IT HAPPEN

Helping students gain confidence in a brighter future is incremental. So never get discouraged if you don't see fast progress. Remember that when you help them expand their vision, they will gradually develop a more optimistic view. The following are some suggestions:

• **Help release the imagination of students.** Ask your students to play the game "What If?" Very simply, ask them to imagine something they would like to see themselves doing in the future. They can pick the time—next week or in ten years. Now invite them to ask themselves, "What if I could really do that? What if it could actually happen?" Maybe someone wants to be an astronaut someday. You then ask the students what they see. Ask them to describe it to the class. Then ask the students to identify some biographies of real astronauts on the Web and ask the student to read and report on these. You can also ask a specific "What if?" question, such as, "What if we all got 100 percent on the next test?" Then you follow up with "What would it take for us to accomplish this?" It is all about helping students release their imagination, become more creative, think new thoughts, and see a new vision of what they can do and what they might become.

• **Help students extinguish the negative.** Explain to students that negative talk of any kind is not welcome in the classroom and that you have a way of getting rid of it. You could don a gas mask or put on some ski goggles, get a can of aerosol air freshener, approach a student, and ask, "So have you heard any negative talk around here?" The student responds by saying, for example, "I hate reading," or "Do we *have* to do this?" and you spray the air freshener and respond, "Extinguish that negative talk." You repeat this several times to make the point that you and all the students are literally going to get rid of negative self-talk and negative talk about others—any kind of negative talk about anything. It just won't be a part of your class. This works as well with teachers as it does with students. Negative talk is pervasive. Sometimes it is subtle and other times it's blatant. However, it is usually hovering around in schools and other organizations.

- **Help students make no excuses.** Students are masters at making excuses. Adults have had longer to develop the skill, so they are often even better. The best way to deal with excuses is to raise awareness of what excuses are. A student walks into class and says, "I couldn't do the assignment because my dad was using his computer, and I couldn't get on it." You respond, "Sounds like an excuse, don't you think?" In her mind, the student was simply stating a fact, so you need to teach that simple statements of fact, even when they're true, if they are used to excuse us from doing what we needed to do, are excuses. For example, "It was too cold," or "I couldn't stay awake," or "I forgot my book, so I couldn't read the assignment": You can turn these statements into questions and show students how they are nothing more than excuses. They chose to forget. They chose to avoid the assignment rather than solving the problem and finding another way to do it. If you work on excuse making openly and often, students will remember their work more often, and they will stop making excuses for poor performance.

- **Exude confidence in achieving a new vision.** Whether in a school or in any other organization, the leader or teacher needs to exude confidence that a particular unachieved vision can be realized. Use the *Spyglass* story with your class. Ask students what they envision. Share with them what you envision. Tell them that you know absolutely that they can achieve this vision. Explain how you will mark the pathway to the vision (perhaps visually on a bulletin board) and how they will help you track progress toward the vision. Show them how each one is necessary for the vision to be achieved. It's a group goal, not an individual goal. That means all students will need to be working their way toward the unrealized vision for the class.

8

Choose to Lead

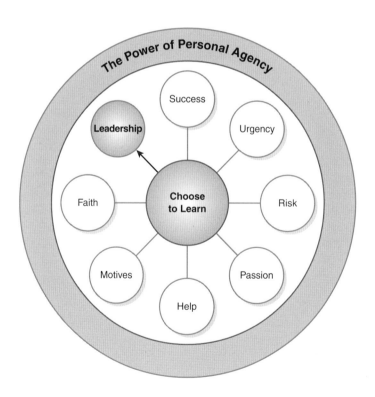

W hen a learner's fire begins to burn, that person cannot be restrained from learning. The need to understand the topic at hand is much more than a personal interest. Interests are nice to satisfy, but what we are talking about is an absolute necessity to know, to be able to do something that has to be done.

When the learning fire begins to burn, it is relatively small—not very hot—but as the fire gets fed, the flames increase in size and intensity. When the fire grows to a certain level, the learner feels compelled to share the newly found knowledge or skill. As Walter Gong, a professor of education, taught: the learner begins to teach it to others (see Covey, 2005). Then, as the fire continues to grow even brighter, the learner extends the teaching to still others. The learner begins to lead. Leadership, like teaching, is all about building fires in those we serve (see Crowther, Ferguson, Kaagan, & Hann, 2002; Gabriel, 2005).

Lighting a fire is more than responding to the interest of the learner. It's creating an interest where no interest existed. That means that the teacher must find a way to show the learner that the task to be learned is absolutely essential in the life of the learner—not that it's nice to know but that the learner cannot live any longer without it.

I recently gave a presentation on the Three D's of Success to a large, mixed-age group. Ten days later a faculty member at the university approached me to tell me that he had heard the presentation and had appreciated it:

> You might want to know that a week after your presenta-
> tion, I was teaching a group of fifteen-year-olds and asked
> them if anyone could remember the "Three D's" from
> your talk. And they could. They chimed in, "desire, deci-
> sion, and determination."

The impressive thing to me about this faculty member was that he did not feel satisfied with his own learning of the

Three D's. He wanted to share the idea with those he was teaching. He was demonstrating to those young people that when new learning occurs, you share it. You don't just keep it inside for yourself. You give it away to help someone else.

Every chapter in this book has implications for leadership, as well as for learning and teaching. The Three D's apply to leaders as well as to learners and teachers. A principal of a school, a district administrator, or even a parent can apply the Three D's as they attempt to lead those within their steward-ship. The leader has a desire to reach a goal, just as a learner has such a desire. However the learner's desire might be indi-vidual, focusing on a specific topic or skill the learner is trying to master. The leader obviously sets goals too, but the leader's goals expand to an organization. It is one thing for an indi-vidual to go after a personal goal. It's quite another for an organization to collectively pursue a goal.

But whether the goal is individual or collective, the Three D's apply equally well. In the case of the organization, the whole group must want to achieve the goal. If they have no desire to achieve it, it will not happen. But desire is not enough. They must also collectively decide to pursue the goal. In the case of a school, all members of the faculty must decide to help students improve their reading scores. Gaining con-sensus, even on the simplest of goals, can be challenging for the leader, but the leader who chooses to learn will focus on consensus building until the organization can make a firm decision to achieve a worthy goal.

Once all participants have decided that they want to achieve the goal, the leader needs to help them acquire the skills and knowledge necessary to succeed. They will do things they've never done before—which can be unsettling for some, even paralyzing for others. So the leader needs to pro-vide the right kind of help at the right time in the right way. If people feel pushed or forced, resistance will likely increase, and the goal will not be reached. If participants feel supported and valued, progress toward the goal will happen.

WHO SHOULD LEAD?

Most think of leadership as a title or position—for example, principal, superintendent, president, vice president—but title alone has little to do with real leadership. Leadership is offering new ideas that move the organization forward. It is, in one sense, a form of gift giving (Osguthorpe & Patterson, 1998). Everyone in an organization can give something to help the group progress. Ideas must be learned and lived before they can be used to help others move forward. A teacher might come up with a new strategy for teaching writing to fifth graders, but that strategy—before it will be of worth to others—must be proven effective. The teacher needs to master it and then live it. Then, if it helps, the teacher can offer it to others.

So the answer to the question "Who should lead?" is *everyone.* Everyone needs to lead. However, if people are unwilling to try something they've never done before or cannot muster the determination to master the necessary skills or succumb to any one of the many addictions to failure, they will be unable to lead. If, however, they choose to learn in the way we have described in this book, they will naturally lead because they will have ideas that must be shared.

The pattern that emerges is simple: choose to learn, choose to teach, choose to lead. When people choose to learn, they also choose to teach, and as soon as they enter the teaching realm, they are leading because they are giving someone else a new skill or bit of knowledge that changes them in some way and helps them succeed at something they thought was impossible.

LEADING AND HELPING

The three kinds of help we have discussed—*help that invites, help that instructs, and help that confirms*—apply to leadership as much as to learning and teaching. A leader invites group members to see a vision, believe in that vision, and seek to achieve the vision. It is a process of attraction and invitation. Leaders who master the art of invitation move their organizations forward. Those who don't master this art become addicted to failure, blaming their lack of success on the stubbornness of those they were assigned to lead.

If the leader can successfully invite participants to pursue the same goal, then the instructional help begins. The leader identifies new skills that will be necessary to realize the vision of the organization and provides instructional guidance and help to ensure that all participants understand their role in moving the organization forward.

Finally, when the group is developing expertise and becoming determined to reach the goal, the leader must provide help that confirms. Each individual, whether the person is in a classroom or a Fortune 500 company, sees things from a personal point of view—not from the organizational view. Someone might say, "I feel like the organization is doing well because I'm really doing well." Or another might say, "I've had a bad month, so I think the whole organization has had a bad month." When people don't have access to all the data—which they seldom do—they jump to conclusions that are often incorrect.

So the leader must enter the picture and set things straight. The leader must provide help that confirms. This means, just as in the classroom, finding evidence of progress and showing everyone in the organization that this progress is being made. Good leaders build on the strengths of the organization. They emphasize positive data and diminish negative data.

PERCEPTION AND LEADERSHIP

Effective leaders are not easily discouraged. They can't be. Because the minute they become negative, the black cloud spreads throughout the whole organization. Participants might say, "I thought we were doing worse, and now I know we are." Once this doomsaying sets in, the downward spiral accelerates. The reality of the situation doesn't really matter. If people in the organization perceive that things are getting worse, things will get worse. If people think that things are getting better, they will build on those positive aspects, and things will get better.

Perception is always more important than reality. How people perceive their environment is more important than the actual condition of things around them because perception determines conduct. People don't act on reality. They act on their perceptions of reality. So leaders and teachers must understand how people are perceiving things around them, not just the actual condition of those things. A participant might perceive that the goal of the organization is unachievable. Regardless of how achievable it actually is, the goal will not be reached unless participants come to perceive that it is achievable.

One of the most common weaknesses in perception is that participants in an organization view the person with a leadership title as the one solely responsible to lead. Whether they are students in a classroom or teachers in a school or principals in a district, they wait for their superior to give the marching orders, and then they respond. They view leading as *directing* others, but this perceptual frame limits the whole organization. Another view of leadership—one that relies on learning rather than on control or power—is a view that emphasizes the offering of new ideas. This is the gift that everyone in an organization has to offer the larger group: new ideas, ideas that will move the organization forward. Some have called these types of organizations "learning organizations" (Pettinger, 2002).

Those who describe learning organizations are typically talking of businesses, but institutions that should be the most skilled of all learning organizations should be schools and universities. This means that schools and universities should be malleable, open to change, and responsive to data that show a need for change. Many associated with schools and universities may not use these characteristics to describe the organizations in which they work. The organizations are often seen as rigid, slow to change, and unresponsive to new data. Why? Not to oversimplify, but we see it as a lack of choosing to learn. A learning organization must consciously choose to learn. It must be interested in its own performance and determined to improve. Otherwise it will remain as it is.

Choosing to learn has a very focused meaning for individual students and teachers. This focused meaning has been a primary aim of this book. The broader meaning of choosing to learn applies to whole systems and organizations—the classroom; the school; and the district, state, and federal systems of education. Our assertion is that individuals are not the only ones who can become addicted to failure. Whole organizations can also fall prey to this subtle undermining force to be satisfied with mediocrity.

We do not pretend that helping whole organizations choose to learn is an easy process or a quick one. We are convinced, however, because of our own lived experience that it is possible. To achieve it, all participants in the organization need to change their perception of who they are and what their role is. They need to choose to learn, take responsibility to teach others what they have learned, and then choose to lead. It can be a seamless, natural process, but it must be fostered by more than the leader at the top. All those with titles need to see their role as helping each person in their stewardship become a leader. All individuals need to develop a desire to give the gifts to the organization that each was meant to give. Then, as each new idea emerges, is considered, refined, and implemented, the organization progresses, because each individual within the organization is progressing. They are choosing to learn.

MAKING IT HAPPEN

Your organization is the focal point of this section, but the focus goes in two directions. The teacher, for example, might think the organization is the classroom, but also the school in which that classroom resides. The principal might think first of the school but also of the district, the district administrator of the district office but also of the state office, and the state official of the state office but also of the federal system. Leaders with titles think first of the organization for which they are responsible. Then they think of the organization to which they might offer their gifts of ideas.

• **The three-person problem.** Walter Gong taught that the "simplest case" of education is three people, not two (Covey, 2005). Most think of one teacher and one student as the most basic form of education, but Professor Gong said that it was actually one teacher, one student, and then another student taught by the student who just learned something. The adage went something like this: You have not really learned anything until you have taught it to someone else. Try using this approach in your classroom. When students learn new skills, invite them to teach those skills to others. You can orchestrate it in your own classroom, school, or district. When a teacher becomes expert at a new teaching methodology, invite that teacher to train others in its use.

• **Invite all participants to share ideas.** Foster the informal sharing of new ideas in teacher meetings or in individual classrooms of students. Celebrate the offering of ideas as an organizational imperative. Make certain that everyone knows that ideas are being generated throughout the organization, not just by leaders with titles. Give examples of ideas that are moving the organization forward and then invite participants to generate like ideas. Set aside time in the classroom and in professional meetings for brainstorming. Ask participants to come prepared to share ideas they have been thinking about. Use organization-wide Listserves to share the ideas over e-mail. Ask for feedback on the ideas by e-mail or in person. Let the ideas emerge. Then find ways to let others give their reactions to the ideas—the refining process. Finally, develop a plan to implement ideas that participants want to implement.

- **Teach all participants that the power to choose is within them.** Most participants hesitate to assert themselves because they fear that their idea will not be accepted or, even worse, that their idea might make them look incompetent. Ideas are like young plants. They need nurturing so that they can become strong and healthy. Talk with participants—whether they be students, teachers, or administrators—about their personal agency. Share examples that convince participants that they have more internal power than they might think. We're not referring to the power to control others. We are referring to the power to contribute, the power to change, the power to lift the organization to a new level. Ask for participants to express their views—their choices—on everything to do with the organization. Let them suggest changes that they believe will move the organization forward.

- **Everyone helps everyone.** Participants need to understand that for a group to move forward, everyone must contribute, everyone must help each other. Collaborative leadership is the only kind in the end that causes lasting positive improvements. Ideas such as reciprocal teaching give all students an opportunity to read and understand expository grade level material (Palinscar & Brown, 1984). Small groups of students with varying reading abilities teach each other using the four reading skills of summarizing, questioning, clarifying, and predicting. Students at risk are able to learn and remember instead of failing again because they can't comprehend the text.

Epilogue

Expect Success

A young man came to us once for advice. We had been working with him for several months to help him set higher goals than he was accustomed to setting. In the middle of the conversation he looked up with a surprised expression and said, "You are the first ones who have ever expected me to succeed." He seemed sad and happy at the same moment—sad because he was beginning to realize that he had missed out on so much in the past and happy because the future suddenly looked brighter.

Someone may read this book and say that it is about education. Another may read it and say that it is about success. Both readers will be correct, but the central message of the book—the message that ties everything together and gives life to each of the principles—can be summed up in the first word of the book's title: *choose*. This book is about learning and teaching, but it is about a special kind of learning and teaching in which both learner and teacher *choose* to succeed.

We are confident that if we had spoken to the parents of the young man who came to us for advice, they would have said that they had always expected their son to succeed. If we had asked some of his friends, they would have agreed that the young man was doing just fine, but he did not perceive it that way. He did not view himself as one who could be successful at almost anything. Those around him did not view him as a failure, but he knew somewhere inside that he was falling below his potential. He just needed someone who expected him to do more. Then he could come to embrace those same expectations. He could choose to learn.

Collins (2005), in his book *Good to Great: Why Some Companies Make the Leap and Others Don't,* introduces the hedgehog principle. Effective leaders who select and articulate a single, unifying big idea are like the hedgehog in the ancient Greek parable. After selecting the big idea, they become passionate about achieving it. They exercise their personal agency to choose what the organization most needs.

The fox in the parable has a hard time choosing. He comes up with a different strategy to attack the hedgehog, but the hedgehog is completely undeterred because he knows he has a foolproof defense. The hedgehog expects success. He has exercised his agency and has chosen what works. The fox, we suggest, is addicted to failure. He has a hard time choosing, and so he keeps doing what doesn't work. After so many failed attempts, he likely does not expect success.

Similarly, in the book *The Influencer: The Power to Change Anything* the authors emphasize that those who bring about important changes in the world—those who solve the seemingly unsolvable problems—choose to have influence (Patterson, Grenny, Switzler, & McMillan, 2007). They choose to lead. Like the leaders in the companies that become great, influencers increase their power of choice. They expect to succeed.

So if the ability of individuals and groups to exercise their power of choice is at the heart of improving the human condition, how does one person help another to increase this power? Schools that are good but not great don't see themselves as failures, because in one sense they're not. They reach their benchmarks each year. They avoid being penalized by the district or state. People who do not become effective "influencers" or leaders, but who live passable lives, likewise do not see themselves as failures, and in many ways they're not. They pay their bills. They go to work. They contribute to their communities.

But our definition of success and failure is meant to cause discomfort for those who are just doing okay. To get from good to great as an individual or as an organization, individuals need to expand their personal agency. To solve the seemingly unsolvable problem, an influencer must focus on an overarching goal that will lead to success—reaching one's full potential. That is success in our definition. Failure, that great impostor, is nothing more than falling short of what one could be. It's a failure to choose that keeps eating away at one's personal power to choose in the future.

In our definition the great corporation, the great school, the great person is always in jeopardy of failing, because success is a moving target. There is always some worthy, almost impossible goal hovering out there somewhere in the future. Choosing to avoid the goal is failure, no matter how much praise or profit may come.

Becoming aware of one's potential and of the goals that one needs to accomplish is a cycle that can cause an increase in one's power to choose. It's all about awareness. The young man who told us that no one had ever expected him to succeed was becoming aware of his own power to choose and of goals that were worth pursuing. He was waking up to his own potential to take control of his life and not settle for simply *coping* with problems that seemed unsolvable and goals that seemed unreachable (see Patterson et al., 2007).

Like most types of learning, developing a greater power of personal choice demands practice. Every time people choose to learn, every time people choose to tackle a truly daunting task and stay with it until they succeed, they will increase their power of personal agency, their power to choose. This is the central message of this book, a message we believe can help anyone become a better learner or teacher and enjoy a happier life.

References

American Heart Association. (2007). Smoking cessation. Retrieved October 4, 2007, from http://www.americanheart.org/presenter .jhtml?identifier=4731

Arbinger Institute. (2002). *Leadership and self-deception: Getting out of the box.* San Francisco: Berrett-Koehler.

Baker, J. (1999). Teacher-student interaction in urban at-risk classrooms: Differential behavior, relationship quality, and student satisfaction with school. *The Elementary School Journal, 100*(1), 55–70.

Bandura, A. (1994). Self-efficacy. In V. S. Ramachaudran (Ed.), *Encyclopedia of human behavior* (Vol. 4, pp. 71–81). New York: Academic Press.

Bandura, A. (1997). *Self-efficacy: The exercise of control.* New York: W. H. Freeman and Company.

Bedley, T. (2007). Teaching elementary school. Retrieved October 10, 2007, from http://www.timbedley.com

Benard, B. (1995). Fostering resilience in children. Urbana, IL: ERIC

Bloom, B. S. (1974). Time and learning, *American Psychologist, 29*(9), 682–688.

Collins, J. (2005). *Good to great: Why some companies make the leap and others don't.* New York: Harper-Collins.

Collins, L. M. (2007, October 9). Genetics giant: U professor wins Nobel Prize in medicine. *Deseret Morning News*, Salt Lake City, UT, pp. A1, A4.

Cooperrider, D. L., & Whitney, D. (2005). *Appreciative inquiry: A positive revolution in change.* San Francisco, CA: Berrett and Koehler.

Covey, S. R. (2004). *The seven habits of highly effective people.* New York: Free Press.

Covey, S. R. (2005). *The eighth habit: From effectiveness to greatness.* New York: Simon & Schuster.

Crowther, F., Ferguson, M., Kaagan, S. S., & Hann, L. (2002). *Developing teacher leaders: How teacher leadership enhances school success,* Thousand Oaks, CA: Sage Publications.

Dweck, C. S. (2006). *Mindset: The new psychology of success*, New York: Random House.

Evans, R. I. (1989). *Albert Bandura: The man and his ideas.* New York: Praeger.

Evans, R. P. (2000). *The spyglass.* New York: Simon & Schuster.

Evenbeck, S., & Hamilton, S. (2006). From "my course" to "our program." *Peer Review, 8*(3), 17.

Feldman, K. (1988). Effective college teaching from the student's and faculty's view: Matched or mismatched priorities? *Research in Higher Education, 28*(4), 291–344.

Gabriel, J. S. (2005). *How to thrive as a teacher leader.* Baltimore: Association for Supervision and Curriculum Development.

Gagné, R. M. (1985). *The conditions of learning and theory of instruction.* New York: Holt, Rinehart and Winston.

Gardner, H. (2006). *Multiple intelligences: New horizons in theory and practice.* New York: Perseus.

Greene, M. (2000). *Releasing the imagination: Essays on education, the arts, and social change.* San Francisco: Jossey-Bass.

Hancock, L. (2007, October 27). CSI: Young sleuths follow crime trail. *Deseret Morning News*, pp. B1–B2.

Hansen, D. T. (2001). *Exploring the moral heart of teaching: Toward a teacher's creed.* New York: Teachers College Press.

Hedegaard, M. (2005). The zone of proximal development as basis for instruction. In H. Daniels (Ed.), *An introduction to Vygotsky* (2nd ed., pp. 227–252). London: Psychology Press.

Hinckley, G. B. (1986). The continuing pursuit of truth. *Ensign*, Salt Lake City, UT, Church of Jesus Christ of Latter-day Saints, 2–4.

Inouye, D., Merrill, P. F., & Swan, R. H. (2004). Help: Toward a new ethics-centered paradigm for instructional design and technology, *IDT Record.* Retrieved September 5, 2007, from http://www.indiana.edu/~idt/

Johansson, T., & Kroksmark, T. (2004). Teachers' intuition-in-action: How teachers experience action. *Reflective Practice, 5*(3), 357–381.

King, M. L. (1963, August 28). *I have a dream.* Retrieved January 5, 2008, from http://www.americanrhetoric.com/speeches/mlkihaveadream.htm

Krathwohl, J. R. (1989). Attitudes and affect in learning and instruction. *Educational media international, 26*(2), 85–100.

Madsen, T. (1978). *The highest in us.* Salt Lake City, UT: Bookcraft.

Mager, R. F., & Pipe, P. (1997). *Analyzing performance problems, or you really oughta wanna: How to figure out why people aren't doing what they should be and what to do about it.* Atlanta, GA: Center for Effective Performance.

Morales, C. (2007, August 11). His car fell 65 feet into the Mississippi River. *Deseret Morning News, LDS Church News, 158*(58).

Muller, C. (2001). The role of caring in the teacher-student relationship for at-risk students. *Sociological Inquiry, 71*(2), 241–255.

Nelson, H. G., & Stolterman, E. (2003). *The design way: Intentional change in an unpredictable world.* Englewood Cliffs, NJ: Educational Technology Publications.

Newman, B. M., & Newman, P. R. (2005). *Development through life: A psychosocial approach.* Boston: Wadsworth.

Noddings, N., & Shore, P. J. (1999). *Awakening the inner eye: Intuition in education.* Troy, NY: Educators International Press.

Osguthorpe, R. D (in press). On the reasons we want teachers of good disposition and moral character. *Journal of Teacher Education.*

Osguthorpe, R. T. (1996). *The education of the heart: Rediscovering the spiritual roots of learning.* American Fork, UT: Covenant Communications.

Osguthorpe, R. T. (1997). The power of the arts to edify. In D. R. Walling (Ed.), *Under construction: The role of the arts and humanities in postmodern schooling* (pp. 119–135). Bloomington, IN: Phi Delta Kappa Educational Foundation.

Osguthorpe, R. T., & Harrison, G. V. (1976). The effects of preremedial instruction on low achievers' math skills and classroom participation. *Reading Improvement, 13*(3), 147–150.

Osguthorpe, R. T., & Patterson, R. S. (1998). *Balancing the tensions of change: Eight keys to collaborative educational renewal.* Thousand Oaks, CA: Corwin Press.

Palinscar, A., & Brown, A. (1984). Reciprocal teaching of comprehension-fostering and comprehension-monitoring activities. *Cognition and instruction, 1*(2), 117–175.

Palmer, P. (1997). *The courage to teach: Exploring the inner landscape of a teacher's life.* San Francisco: Jossey-Bass.

Patterson, K., Grenny, J., Switzler, A., & McMillan, R. (2007). *Influencer: The power to change anything.* Columbus, OH: McGraw-Hill.

Pettinger, R. (2002). *The learning organization,* Hoboken, NJ: John Wiley & Sons.

Purkey, W. W. (2000). *What students say to themselves: Internal dialogue and school success.* Thousand Oaks, CA: Sage Publications.

Purkey, W. W. (2002). *Becoming an invitational leader: A new approach to personal and professional success.* Lake Worth, FL: Humanics.

Rainer, P. (2007, March 23). Pride gets into the swim of things. *Christian Science Monitor.* Retrieved September 20, 2007, from http://www.csmonitor.com.

Romano, L. (2005, December 25). Literacy of college graduates is on decline: Survey's finding of a drop in reading proficiency is inexplicable, experts say. *Washington Post,* A12.

Russo, R. (2007, August 19). Pre-season champ: USC voted team to beat in first AP poll, *Deseret Morning News*, p. D9.

Scardamalia, M., & Bereiter, C. (2006). Knowledge building: Theory, pedagogy, and technology. In R. K. Sawyer (Ed.), *The Cambridge handbook of the learning sciences* (pp. 97–118). London: Cambridge University Press.

Schaler, J. A. (2000). *Addiction is a choice*. Chicago: Open Court.

Schneider, M. (2007). National assessment of educational progress: The nation's report card: Reading 2007 and the nation's report card: Mathematics 2007. Retrieved July 10, 2007, from http://nces.ed.gov/whatsnew/commissioner/remarks2007/9_25_2007.asp.

Schön, D. A. (1983). *The reflective practitioner*. New York: Basic Books.

Swan, R. H. (2008). Deriving operational principles for the design of engaging learning experiences. Doctoral dissertation, Brigham Young University, Provo, UT.

Top, B., & Osguthorpe, R. T. (1985). College students' perceptions of their most fulfilling and most frustrating learning experiences. *College Student Journal, 19*(3), 222–226.

Van Manen, M. (1990). *Researching lived experience: Human science for an action sensitive pedagogy*. Albany: SUNY Press.

Waitley, D. (1985). *The winner's edge*. New York: Penguin.

Warner, C. T. (2001). *Bonds that make us free: Healing our relationships, coming to ourselves*. Salt Lake City, UT: Shadow Mountain.

Westerman, D. A. (1990). A study of expert and novice teacher decision making: An integrated approach. (ERIC Document Reproduction Service No. ED322128)

Index